The Sound That Perceives the World

The Sound That Perceives the World

Calling Out to the Bodhisattva

KOSHO UCHIYAMA

Foreword by SHOHAKU OKUMURA

Translated by HOWARD LAZZARINI with SHOHAKU OKUMURA and SHOKO HAYASHI LAZZARINI

Wisdom Publications
132 Perry Street
New York, NY 10014 USA
wisdom.org

Library of Congress Cataloging-in-Publication Data is available.
LCCN 2025004961

ISBN 978-1-61429-951-6   ebook ISBN 978-1-61429-975-2

29 28 27 26 25   5 4 3 2 1

Cover design by Marc Whitaker.. Interior design by Michael Russem. Typeset by Tim Holtz.

Printed on acid-free paper that meets the guidelines for permanence and durability of the Production Guidelines for Book Longevity of the Council on Library Resources.

Printed in the United States of America.

Please visit fscus.org.

Contents

Foreword

I know there are many people who cannot practice Zen meditation (zazen) even though they want to, because of various reasons: busy life, sickness, or aging. When it is not possible to practice zazen, there might be something else we can do.

Now I am seventy-four years old, and because of my physical condition associated with aging, I haven't been able to practice zazen since last year. I had been practicing zazen for more than fifty years, since I was nineteen years old. These days, walking is my practice. Since I was young, walking has been a meditation practice for me. Almost every day, I just walk, opening the hand of thought.

Now I can walk, but eventually, it might be that I cannot even walk. As practicing Buddhists, we need to be creative and find something we can do as a religious practice instead of sitting zazen. For my teacher, Kosho Uchiyama Roshi, that was letting go of thought and wholeheartedly chanting *Namu Kanzeon Bosatsu* (literally, "I take refuge in Kanzeon Bodhisattva").

In this book, Uchiyama Roshi describes his difficult experiences during World War II, through which he began to find the meaning of the practice of chanting the name of Avalokiteshvara (Kanzeon in Japanese), and the process of studying the meaning of chanting practice. His conclusion is that chanting the name of Kanzeon, *Namu Kanzeon Bosatsu* is the same as other kinds of Buddhist practices such as zazen and chanting *nenbutsu*—that is, *Namu Amida Butsu* (I am grateful for the vow of Amitabha Buddha to create a Pure Land where all beings can manifest liberation). That is why he made the subtitle for the original book "Practice of the East" (東洋の行). He wrote, "Even though it is buried in the dust and dirt in the half-broken temples, and it is difficult to evaluate it as a treasure, it is nothing other than the final place to return in our life."

Dogen Zenji used the expression "the final place to return in our life" (or more literally, "ultimate place of return") in *Shobogenzo Kie Bupposobo* ("Taking Refuge in the Buddha, Dharma, and Sangha"). This expression means that the Three Treasures are the final place to which we return.

Uchiyama Roshi's teacher, Kodo Sawaki Roshi, expressed this in modern Japanese as "to live in the way in which we have returned to where we should return." In other words, Buddhism is a religion that teaches us how to live in the way in which we have returned to where we should return, instead of a lackadaisical, lukewarm, cheating, and incomplete way of life.[1] In this context, practicing zazen is no different from chanting the name of Amitabha Buddha or Kanzeon. These practices allow us to return to the original truth our lives are based on—that is, the true reality of all beings: impermanence, no-self, and interconnection. Then we are released from a life based on delusional self-clinging.

Another meaning for the practice of chanting *Namu Kanzeon Bosatsu* for Uchiyama Roshi was that this practice could be done when he could not sit zazen. As he wrote, he found the meaning of chanting *Namu Kanzeon Bosatsu* when he could not practice zazen during World War II, but also, after the war had ended, he sometimes could not practice zazen because of his physical condition. Because he had had tuberculosis since his early twenties, Uchiyama Roshi was physically weak and often in poor health. That was the reason he had to retire when he was sixty-three years old. He could not sit *sesshin* with us for the final two years before his retirement. When he was unable to sit zazen, he chanted *Namu Kanzeon Bosatsu* as his practice. He said zazen is *Namu Kanzeon Bosatsu* practiced with our entire body and mind, and chanting *Namu Kanzeon Bosatsu* is zazen practiced with mouth and mind.

1. See Kosho Uchiyama and Shohaku Okumura, *The Zen Teaching of Homeless Kodo* (Somerville, MA: Wisdom Publications, 2014), 15–17.

This book, which he titled *Kannongyo wo Ajiwau* (Appreciating the Avalokiteshvara Sutra) is one of Uchiyama Roshi's early writings. He originally wrote the chapters of this book as a series of articles for *Hensho*, the newsletter of Myogenji Temple in Nagoya, from 1958 to 1960. This book was published by Hakujusha in 1968. In 1986, Uchiyama Roshi revised the book, removing the final chapter, adding a new chapter, and including his *teisho* (Dharma talk) on the Ten-Line Avalokiteshvara Sutra given at Muryoji Temple in Nagano in 1985.

I hope this book can be a helpful guide for the people who wish to practice Buddhadharma when they are unable to sit zazen.

I wished to translate this book myself, but I found that I didn't have time, so my old friend from Antaiji Temple, Howard Lazzarini, kindly volunteered to work on this translation. I deeply appreciate his several years of hard work.

Shohaku Okumura
Bloomington, Indiana
July 2022

Translator's Preface

During the last year of World War II, Kosho Uchiyama Roshi, one of the preeminent Zen masters of the twentieth century, was eking out a living making charcoal for sale in the mountains of Shimane Prefecture on the coast of Japan. Frigid winds from Siberia blew across the Sea of Japan, dumping deep snows on the mountains in Shimane and often making for whiteout conditions in the mountains and forests where he and his fellow monks harvested raw wood to convert and sell as charcoal. Winter temperatures there were extremely cold, and Roshi and his companions had not come prepared for these conditions; they lacked warm clothing and proper footwear. To make matters worse, food was scarce, so they were forced to ration what little they had, and they often ate it uncooked, as there was precious little fuel for cooking and heating their meager attic room.

Early one cold morning, as Roshi was trying to prepare some food before the day's work, he looked out the door. It was snowing heavily, but they could not afford to take the day off. He knew they would have to go out into the mountains carrying their heavy tools and equipment. One slip in the snow could mean a fall down the mountainside or slipping from a narrow single log bridge into a frozen creek. Wielding heavy axes and saws with numb hands and fingers could result in a severe injury. As he thought more about his situation, a dark gloom descended on him, and he was overtaken with fear and anxiety. Without thinking, he suddenly started calling out *Namu Kanzeon Bosatsu*, which means "I take refuge in the Bodhisattva Kanzeon." He repeatedly called it out, and after some time his anxiety and feelings of foreboding lessened, and he felt largely relieved of his suffering. For Uchiyama, with a master's degree in Western philosophy from Tokyo's prestigious Waseda University, this was an odd and mysterious experience. Though he had been exposed to the Kannon-gyo, or Avalokiteshvara Sutra, as a child listening to his mother chant the sutra, he had never given serious thought to the words or to the act of calling out to the bodhisattva Kannon when in distress.

After this profound experience, he wrote to his mother and asked her to send him a copy of the Kannon-gyo so that he could stuff it in his robe pocket and read it whenever he had a break in making charcoal. This began his lifelong quest to understand the Kannon-gyo and the power of silently chanting. Until his death he practiced zazen and, when he was unable to sit due to illness, he engaged in the practice of silently chanting.

This book is a translation from Japanese to English of Uchiyama Roshi's book *Appreciating the Kannon-gyo* published in 1986. It is the culmination of over fifty years of Uchiyama Roshi's practice and contemplation of this sutra. However, not only does he seek to interpret this sutra for us, but he also endeavors to shed light on Pure Land practice and his own unique interpretation of the teachings of Jesus and Christianity, and how they relate to his practice of Dogen's *shikantaza* (just sitting). His ecumenical approach to religion is an outgrowth of his lifelong search for truth. His legacy is his practice, his students, his many books on zazen and Buddhist practice written in easy-to-understand language, and his commentaries on Dogen's writings and Buddhist sutras such as the Kannon-gyo. It was my honor and privilege to have met him and to have had him as a teacher. At seventy-four years old, I am pleased to be able to realize my vow to translate a work of Uchiyama Roshi. It has taken me fifty years, but I can now finally feel that I have perhaps done something before I die to further the legacy of two of the most important Zen teachers of the millennium, Kodo Sawaki Roshi and Kosho Uchiyama Roshi.

Acknowledgments

The book couldn't have happened without the help of many individuals. First of all, my wife, Shoko Hayashi Lazzarini, provided invaluable and patient assistance in understanding Uchiyama Roshi's colloquial Japanese. I consider her to be a co-translator.

Without the patient assistance of Shohaku Okumura Roshi, this book would not have been possible. His constant encouragement, inspiring teaching, numerous corrections, and patient help in interpreting Uchiyama Roshi's thought and words were invaluable. I offer him my deepest gratitude and *gassho*. Any translations of Dogen's writings that appear in the text are derived from his previously published translations or translations that have yet to be published.

I had valuable professional editing assistance from the late Elizabeth Kenney in Kyoto. She was a student of Doyu Takamine Roshi. I owe a great deal to her editing skills and her ability to render my translated expressions into concise and crisp English. Her knowledge of Buddhist doctrine was invaluable and informed the text. I offer deep thanks to her memory.

In addition, I would like to thank Arthur and Hiroko Braverman for their help with translating and understanding Pure Land doctrines and practice. Arthur also encouraged me to continue this project and would not let me give up. Daitsu Tom Wright, a renowned translator of Uchiyama Roshi's books and a fellow disciple and a friend of many years, helped with the translation of the Ten-Line Avalokiteshvara Sutra, as well as with his recollections of his visits to Uchiyama Roshi in the years after Roshi retired from Antaiji. Shusoku Kushiya, an assistant to Uchiyama Roshi after his retirement from Antaiji, provided valuable information on Roshi's health and chanting practice. I am grateful to Carl Bielefeldt, emeritus professor in the religious studies department at Stanford, for his assistance in translating from Chinese the outline of the Kannon-gyo by Master Tiantai Zhiyi, which appears in chapter 5.

Rev. Dr. Takashi Miyaji, a professor at the Institute of Buddhist Studies in Berkeley, California, helped me understand Pure Land and Jodo Shinshu doctrine. I consulted Bill "Red Pine" Porter when I had questions about Chinese characters and their original Chinese Buddhist meanings. He always responded immediately to my emails and phone calls. Thank you. My old friend, the *nanga* artist and Zen student Michael Hofmann, also offered valuable suggestions on wording. I would also like to thank Steve Yenik of Kyoto, one of the first translators of Uchiyama Roshi, for his suggestion to avoid a literal translation and trust my own words when the meaning was unclear. I would also like to thank Dr. Randy Reimer for helping me understand the long-term effects of tuberculosis on Uchiyama Roshi's health.

I would like to thank Wisdom Publications for their permission to use chapter 25 of Gene Reeves's excellent translation of the *Lotus Sutra*, which appears in appendix 1. Also, deep thanks to Ben Gleason, my editor at Wisdom, for his excellent suggestions and edits, which refined my text and helped to clarify the many difficult passages.

I also owe a debt of gratitude to the Everett Zazen Group, Chad Freeman, Rachel McGovern, Asao Sakakibara, and Ann Bauleke, for reading through the manuscript during our Zoom reading group meetings, and for all their valuable suggestions.

Finally, I would like to offer my gratitude to my professors at UC Berkeley. Specifically, my profound appreciation and thanks go to Lewis Lancaster, Emeritus Professor of the Department of East Asian Languages, and the late Helen McCollough and the late Francis Motofuji, both professors in the Oriental Languages Department, who fostered my interest in Buddhism and Japanese language and literature.

Of course, any mistakes in translation are solely my responsibility.

I hope this book informs your practice as it has mine.

Howard Lazzarini
Everett, Washington
2023

Translator's Introduction

The Lotus Sutra, Kannon, and the Kannon-gyo

Chapter 25 of the Lotus Sutra is often treated as an independent work called the Avalokiteshvara Sutra, or the Kannon-gyo in Japanese. Before we delve into the Kannon-gyo, it might be useful to lay a foundation by briefly discussing the Lotus Sutra and its seminal role in all branches of Mahayana Buddhist thought.[2] In Burton Watson's introduction to his translation of the Lotus Sutra, he writes that the sutra purports to "represent the highest level of truth, the summation of the Buddha's message."[3] Indeed, throughout China, Korea, Japan, Tibet, and other regions in eastern Asia, the Lotus Sutra is considered one of the most essential texts of Mahayana Buddhism, and has been a major influence on the religions, arts, and letters of those nations.

We do not know where or exactly when the Lotus Sutra was composed.[4] The first translation into Chinese was in 255 CE, but it was a subsequent translation in 406 by the Central Asian scholar-monk Kumarajiva that became the most widely known and is the basis for Gene Reeves's translation of the Kannon-gyo that appears in the appendix. Scholars assume that the translation by Kumarajiva was from an extant Sanskrit text, but that text has been lost.

2. An in-depth discussion of the Lotus Sutra is beyond the scope of this book. For a more comprehensive introduction, see the translator's introductions found in both Burton Watson, trans., *The Lotus Sutra* (New York: Columbia University Press, 1993), x–xxii, and Gene Reeves, trans., *The Lotus Sutra: A Contemporary Translation of a Buddhist Classic* (Somerville, MA: Wisdom Publications, 2008), 1–18.

3. Watson, *Lotus Sutra*, xvii.

4. Watson, *Lotus Sutra*, x

The Lotus Sutra takes place in a fairy-tale world filled with fictional creatures, bodhisattvas with miraculous powers, deities, demons, and other mythical beings. For Western readers (again in Watson's words), "we realize that we have left the world of factual reality far behind."[5] The Kannon-gyo, chapter 25 of the sutra, is titled "The Universal Gateway of the Bodhisattva Regarder of the Cries of the World," and is also part of that fictional world. It begins with the Bodhisattva Inexhaustible Mind asking the Buddha how Regarder of the Cries of the World got that name. The Buddha then explains that he got that name because anyone who wholeheartedly calls out the name of that bodhisattva will be freed from their suffering, no matter what it is.

Kannon, Kanzeon, Guanyin, and Avalokiteshvara

The Sanskrit name for Bodhisattva Regarder of the Cries of the World is Avalokiteshvara, which literally means "the lord who looks down from on high." In Chinese, this bodhisattva is known as Guanyin. Other regions of Asia—including Tibet, Southeast Asia, Sri Lanka, and Korea—each have their own local translation of the name. In Japan, the bodhisattva is called Kannon or Kanzeon. The name Kannon (or Kanzeon) Bosatsu literally means the "bodhisattva who perceives the sounds of the world"—in other words, one who sees and hears the suffering of all sentient beings in this world. I follow Uchiyama Roshi's original text, which sometimes uses Kannon and sometimes Kanzeon. "Kannon-gyo" thus means "Avalokiteshvara Sutra."

Unlike the Buddha or Bodhidharma, Kannon was not an actual historical person. This bodhisattva originated in India and was at first considered male and is still thought of as male in Tibet. In China, Guanyin was originally male but sometime around the twelfth century was transformed by the common people into a female figure.

5. Watson, *Lotus Sutra*, xvi.

In many Asian countries, including Japan, Kannon is revered as a savior deity associated with a sort of folk religion or cult of devotees who worship her and ask for her protection and help, fulfilling a universal human need for relief from suffering. Kannon bears many similarities to the Virgin Mary, inspiring Jesuit missionaries in China to give her the name Goddess of Mercy. A Catholic colleague of mine provided me with the following prayer, which resembles passages in the Kannon-gyo:

> Remember, O most gracious Virgin Mary, that never was it known that anyone who fled to thy protection, implored they help, or sought thy intercession was left unaided. . . . O Mother of the Word Incarnate, despise not my petitions, but in thy mercy hear and answer me.[6]

In the Heart Sutra, it is curious that it is Avalokiteshvara Bodhisattva—Kannon or Kanzeon—instead of the Buddha, who "when deeply practicing *prajnaparamita*, clearly saw that all five aggregates are empty and thus relieved all suffering."[7] Perhaps this is because deep compassion cannot be separated from ultimate wisdom and the bodhisattva vow, which requires a bodhisattva not to enter nirvana until all sentient beings are freed from suffering.

The Kannon-gyo, at first reading, might seem like a kind of fairy tale. For example, one of the first verses in the sutra says, "If anyone who embraces (chants or calls out) the name of Perceiver of the Cries of the World Bodhisattva falls into a great fire, the fire will not burn that person due to the divine authority and power of that bodhisattva."[8] The sutra then goes on to give a list of dire circumstances from which Kannon will free one from if one merely chants or calls out the name.

6. The Memorare prayer, sent to me by Professor Jeanette Rodriguez, Seattle University.

7. The Heart Sutra, San Francisco Zen Center translation.

8. Chapter 25 in Reeves, *Lotus Sutra*, 171.

Uchiyama Roshi and the Kannon-gyo

Uchiyama's adoption of chanting *Namu Kanzeon Bosatsu* (I take refuge in the Bodhisattva Kanzeon) is his own. He practiced both zazen and silently saying Kanzeon's name as the same practice; he was not trying to invoke the Bodhisattva Kanzeon to somehow intercede for him to mystically and miraculously free him from suffering. Rather, zazen and this silent chanting were both practices of "letting go of the hand of thought."[9]

Though Uchiyama's teacher, Sawaki, was certainly influenced by Pure Land Buddhism and probably chanted the nenbutsu, there is no reference to chanting Kanzeon's name in Sawaki's talks. We can't help but remember that Dogen in *Bendowa* ("On the Endeavor of the Way") criticized chanting:

> Intending to reach the Buddha way through stupid ceaseless chanting millions of times is like steering a cart north and trying to go south. It is also the same as trying to put a square peg in a round hole. Reading literature while ignoring the way of practice is like a person reading a prescription but forgetting to take the medicine; what is the benefit? Continuously uttering sounds like frogs in a spring rice paddy croaking day and night is also ultimately worthless.[10]

Though Dogen gave the title "Kannon" to one chapter of *Shobogenzo*, he does not mention the Kannon-gyo at all. When Dogen was in China, he visited Putuoshan Mountain[11] and wrote the following:

9. For an explanation of this expression, see Kosho Uchiyama, *Opening the Hand of Thought: Foundations of Zen Buddhist Practice* (Somerville, MA: Wisdom Publications, 2004).

10. See Kosho Uchiyama Roshi, trans., *The Wholehearted Way: A Translation of Eihei Dogen's* Bendowa (Boston: Tuttle Publishing, 2011), 25–26.

11. Putuoshan is the sacred mountain where Guanyin is said to sit enshrined in a cavelike grotto.

> Guanyin is found amid hearing, considering, practicing, and truly verifying the mind. Why seek the appearance of her sacred face within a cave? I proclaim that pilgrims must themselves awaken. Guanyin does not abide on Potalaka Mountain.[12]

Uchiyama, who was trained in Western philosophy and rationalism,[13] was of course skeptical and didn't pay any serious attention to the Kannon-gyo or chanting the name of Kanzeon before he endured a terrible winter in 1944 in the mountains of Shimane Prefecture. Based on that experience as well as the deaths of two wives—the first, Fueko to tuberculosis, and the second, Chizuko, to pregnancy complications—he struggled for the next fifty years to understand the allegorical meanings of the Kannon-gyo and how this work related to his Buddhist practice and his life. He makes the compelling case for understanding the Kannon-gyo through the lens of the Lotus Sutra, and for using both the Lotus Sutra and Kannon-gyo as the foundation for our life.

However, this book—like all Buddhist teaching—should not be understood as Uchiyama Roshi telling us that we must live exactly as he did. Rather, it is simply an outline of his life and what he himself discovered about the truth of the self (no-self). It is merely a suggestion for us to try to verify with our own experience the practices and wisdom of Buddhism.

Chanting, Saying Quietly, Crying Out, or Singing *Namu Kanzeon Bosatsu*

The Japanese word *tonaeru* can refer to chanting, reciting, saying or speaking, crying out, yelling, shouting, preaching, or singing. In this

12. See verse 45 in Taigen Dan Leighton and Shohaku Okumura, *Dōgen's Extensive Record: A Translation of the Eihei Kōroku* (Somerville, MA: Wisdom Publications, 2010), 621.

13. He held a master's degree in Western philosophy from Tokyo's Waseda University.

translation, I most often use "chanting," but "keeping in mind" or "wholeheartedly chanting" would also be appropriate. Wholeheartedly chanting or saying *Namu Kanzeon Bosatsu* is, for Uchiyama, the same as letting go of thought (often translated as "letting go of the hand of thought")—in other words, just sitting zazen.[14] Uchiyama is saying that in his experience and practice, chanting *Namu Kanzeon Bosatsu* (or the Pure Land nenbutsu) and zazen are the same activity—that is, letting go of thought. In this way, practitioners who cannot physically sit in the zazen posture can still actively practice letting go of thought, even when sick or on their deathbed. This is the most important message of this book.

Uchiyama Roshi's Worldview

Uchiyama died before the internet, smartphones, and other advanced technologies changed how we live. However, he had a universal view of true human progress based on Buddhist principles and his many years of practice, which is crucial for all of us to understand. In his words,

> Human progress is by no means the same as the advancement of natural science; nor does it follow the path of the development of material civilization. Human progress lies in each and every human being becoming an adult.[15]

For him, becoming an adult means living by the bodhisattva vow, watching over others and caring for and helping others. He is urging us to adopt the ideal image of a bodhisattva, protected and guided by zazen and calling out or chanting the Buddha's name, as the true way to bring about real human progress. In this book, Uchiyama explains the

14. When I met Uchiyama at his home, he often said that zazen literally means "letting go of thought," with an accompanying gesture of his hand lifting off the top of his head to indicate a thought flying away.

15. *Opening the Hand of Thought*, 136.

Kannon-gyo as the guiding light for those who seek to understand the bodhisattva ideals and to apply them to their lives.

Uchiyama Roshi and Christianity

Throughout this book, there are many references to the Bible and to Christian ideas. This may be confusing for some, but Uchiyama Roshi did not discriminate between the ideas of Jesus and those of Soto Zen and Pure Land Buddhists. He studied Christianity before he was ordained as a Buddhist priest. According to Daitsu Tom Wright, who originally came to Japan as a Lutheran missionary and whom Uchiyama ordained as a Soto Zen priest and his disciple, Uchiyama encouraged him to continue reading the Bible, particularly Jesus's words, together with his Buddhist practice. Uchiyama was not a practicing Christian in the usual sense, though. Rather, all his life he was a truth seeker. Or, to borrow a phrase from Dogen's *Shobogenzo Genjokoan* ("Actualizing the Fundamental Point"), "To study the Buddha Way is to study the self."[16] He was interested in any philosophical or religious tradition that helped him learn about the true self.

Though he studied the Bible, the life of Jesus, and the history of the Christian church (primarily the Roman Catholic Church), he was not a believer in any institutionalized church. He felt that organized religions, with their authoritarian ecclesiastical hierarchies and belief systems, were far removed from nondualist truth. Also, he felt the institutionalized Christian belief systems were often based on what he called "fairy tales," such as the virgin birth or Christ's resurrection story. Instead, what appealed to him were passages in the Bible such as Mark 9:33, where Christ admonishes his disciples for selfishness and lack of humility:

16. Shohaku Okumura, *Realizing Genjōkōan: The Key to Dōgen's Shōbōgenzō* (Somerville, MA: Wisdom Publications, 2010).

> "Whoever wants to be first must place himself last of all and be servant of all." Then [Christ] took a child and made him stand in front of them. He put his arms round him and said to them, "Whoever welcomes in my name one of these children, welcomes me; and whoever welcomes me, welcomes not only me but also the one who sent me."[17]

For a brief six-month period after the death of his first wife, Uchiyama accepted a position teaching mathematics and philosophy at a small Roman Catholic seminary in Kyushu. During that time, he studied Roman Catholicism with the priests there and considered entering the Catholic priesthood. After six months he decided that he couldn't take that path and resigned his position to return to Tokyo. At that time his father suggested that he go to listen to a talk by Kodo Sawaki Roshi, after which he became Sawaki's student and disciple, and was eventually ordained by him.

Uchiyama Roshi's Health and Death

In the book, Uchiyama describes having serious and potentially life-threatening hemorrhages caused by tuberculosis in his later life. Wondering how the state of his health might have affected him during his many years of practice, I made inquiries of people who were close to Uchiyama at various times. These included telephone conversations, emails, and letters with his students, Shohaku Okumura, Daitsu Tom Wright, and Shusoku Kushiya. Kushiya was Uchiyama Roshi's assistant for many years after he retired from Antaiji Temple, and is most intimately familiar with his health, especially in his later years. Daitsu Tom Wright also made frequent visits to Noke-in, Uchiyama's post-retirement residence.

17. Mark 9:33 (Good News Color Reference Edition).

According to Kushiya, Uchiyama was not strong from his childhood, although it is unknown how much his health affected his early life. It is known, however, that his first wife Fueko, whom he met when they were university students, became ill with tuberculosis and died from the disease in the 1930s, before the availability of antibiotics and other treatments used today. Uchiyama contracted the disease from Fueko, but somehow he recovered. As Okumura told me, the disease became latent in Uchiyama, allowing him to avoid isolation. When Uchiyama was ordained in 1941, he was healthy enough to take part in the severe zazen practice under Sawaki at Daichuji Temple in the mountains of Tochigi Prefecture. This included many multiday sesshins with twenty-four hours of zazen—the monks were only allowed to sleep in the zazen posture from midnight until 2 A.M.

In 1966, Uchiyama became the abbot after Sawaki's death in 1965, and he continued to sit all or part of the sesshins until 1973, when his health deteriorated. Between 1973 and 1975, when he retired, Uchiyama was unable to sit sesshins or give the weekly *teisho*, or Dharma talk.

In the words of Okumura,

> Because of his physical condition, we did not expect him to do anything but take good care of himself. By doing so, we felt that he was providing us with a role model of how to care for ourselves. For us, that was one of his most precious teachings as the abbot of Antaiji.

After Uchiyama retired, he suffered from tuberculosis-related hemorrhages and was diagnosed with tuberculosis of the elderly. It is unfortunately common for patients who have suffered from tuberculosis in their early lives to experience a recurrence of the disease as they age and their immune systems weaken.[18] According to Shusoku Kushiya,

18. Dr. Randy Reimer, MD, in a 2022 discussion with the translator on the epidemiology of tuberculosis.

Uchiyama may have been hospitalized for short periods after these episodes, but mostly his third wife, Keiko,[19] cared for him at his home with the assistance of a physician.

According to Daitsu Tom Wright,

> During the years that I visited him at Noke-in, in Kohata, he was usually bedridden in the spring for two or three months. Sometimes Keiko invited me in, but sometimes she said that he was too ill for me to visit.

On his final day, Uchiyama went out for a walk. When he returned, he collapsed in the entryway and had to be helped back into the house and onto his futon. He chose not to call for emergency medical help or to go to a hospital, but instead the doctor was called to attend him. According to his disciple Doyu Takamine, who arrived at Noke-in in the early evening, Uchiyama died later that evening in Keiko's arms, smiling and saying to her that he had finished his last poem, "Ogamu" ("Bowing with Deep Reverence") earlier that day.[20] What is clear to me is that, even though Uchiyama had serious physical limitations all his life, after his 1941 ordination he persevered in his practice of Buddhism as a disciple of Sawaki and as abbot of Antaiji. Uchiyama Roshi's final poem completed on the day of his death on March 13, 1998, best summarizes his lifelong quest for truth:

19. Prior to his retirement, Uchiyama married his third wife, Keiko, but they agreed to live separately until after his retirement in 1975. She passed away in February 2020.

20. For Tom Wright's translation of the complete poem, see his introduction to Kōshō Uchiyama, *Deepest Practice, Deepest Wisdom* (Somerville, MA: Wisdom Publications, 2018), xxi.

Bowing with Deep Reverence

Joining the right hand with the left—bowing with deep reverence
Becoming one with God and Buddha—bowing with deep reverence
Becoming one with Everything I meet—bowing with deep reverence
Becoming one with the entire myriad things (universe)—bowing with deep reverence
Wholeheartedly joining Life with Life—bowing with deep reverence

Appreciating the Kannon-gyo

Preface

These days we try to manage everything by using science and technology. However, when that doesn't work, we get confused and don't know what to do. For example, when we get sudden news of an airplane crash, or when our doctor tells us that we may have cancer, or even just in the normal course of our lives, it's not unusual to encounter situations that leave us at a loss.

When we feel that everything seems meaningless, we may sink into a feeling of deep depression. When we don't know what to do, or when we seem to have no options, we can fall into an existential crisis or even have a serious nervous breakdown. In our age of science and technology, when we run into a situation that can't be resolved by our human abilities, and religion doesn't provide any answers, we are at our wits end. In response to this, I believe that we need to discover a faith that agrees with our intellect and reason. With that in mind, I have written this book after rereading the ancient Avalokiteshvara Sutra and the Ten-Line Kannon Sutra.

Introduction

What Kind of Religion Is Buddhism?

It seems that nowadays when people encounter the words *Buddhism* or *Buddha*, most want to look the other way. That is probably because for most people the framework of Buddhism as an established religious institution has grown old and decayed and has been abandoned by modern people in Japan. The dilapidated old structure of the Buddhist religion can't be restored to the fresh vitality it once had—and I think there is no need to do so.

But do you know there is a treasure of inestimable worth hidden in this old building? I believe that this treasure should not remain buried in the ruins. Somehow, I hope that younger generations will discover this treasure and make it come alive for generations to come.

What is this great treasure? Though it is buried in the dust and dirt of the ruins of traditional Buddhism, and it is not easy to recognize it as a treasure, it is actually "the final place to return to in our life." This means to take refuge in the Buddha (the historical Shakyamuni Buddha), the Dharma (his teachings on awakening to the reality of life), and the Sangha (the community of people who study the Buddha's teachings and follow his way of life).

Dogen Zenji writes in *Shobogenzo Kie Bupposobo* ("Taking Refuge in the Buddha, Dharma, and Sangha"),

> Question: Why do you take refuge in the Three Treasures?
> Answer: Because these three are the true place to return to (the ultimate refuge).

This expression, "true place to return to," or "ultimate refuge," means finally arriving at the place where we should be. My teacher, Kodo Sawaki Roshi, expressed this concept more simply in modern Japanese: "to live as if having arrived at your life's ultimate destination, or having finally returned to a true way of life." In other words, Buddhism teaches us that this life is our true and final refuge, and so we should not live in some meaningless, selfish, half-baked, irresponsible way.

In the course of human civilization here on earth there has never been any other religion or religious culture that points so purely and directly to the essence of existence. Religions like Christianity are wrapped in mythological doctrine, but nowadays a mythological worldview cannot stand up to scientific principles. Moreover, the god figure is fading from view. In the same way that God has been lost, the Buddhist notion of "living our life having finally returned to a true way of life" has also begun to fade away.

However, in the deep recesses of the ancient temple that is traditional Buddhism—not to be mixed up with the mythology of the Buddha—is the purest and most concrete practice, a Way handed down to us through generations. In any case, I hope to recover this ancient Asian legacy of the Buddha and apply it to our modern lives.

In our current era, we don't think about our own lives as much as we should. As long as we are living as human beings and call ourselves modern people, of course we have some sort of idea about how to live our own lives. But mostly instead of looking at the entirety of our lives, we focus instead only on how to make a living. We see life only in terms of securing our own temporary happiness and ideal living conditions.

Let's look at the idealized "happy" and so-called "complete" life. Most people want to do well in school, get a good job, find the perfect partner, save money to buy the best house, furniture, appliances, car, and so on. In our teens and twenties, we can't think about a future beyond this. At this age, we are caught up in this flowery dream, and the future is just a dim blur. Nevertheless, next we want to work our way up through a career while having kids, who (in this ideal life) also do perfectly in school.

In our thirties and forties, our enthusiasm for this dream begins to dissipate. When we think about what will come next in life, we don't have flowery dreams, but instead a sad and empty feeling somewhere deep down in our hearts. For a while, that sadness and loneliness can be eased by listening to popular songs or watching sports. But what's really happening is that our ability to ponder the future becomes fuzzy.

In any event, assuming that we live past our thirties or forties, life continues. When we reach our fifties and sixties, we need to secure an income for old age and take up a quiet hobby. Then, when grandchildren come along, we do everything we can to make them happy. Then, the life dream of our fifties and sixties is again interrupted. That undeniable feeling of emptiness comes back with a vengeance—no one seems able to overcome it and continue the dream. Rather, we are attacked by this sad and empty feeling, like a typhoon making landfall, which topples our dream of the ideal life and becomes our reality.

After that, naturally the ongoing reality is that we try to enjoy things as much as we can, but our children move out and have lives of their own. Eventually, our partner, whom we have taken along with us for half our life, dies. Suddenly we lose our strength and get high blood pressure. Then there is nothing left but the grave.

I recall the poem, "A flower's life is short, and there is much suffering."

I don't mean to espouse a pessimistic view of life. All I am saying is that if you continue to be guided by this sketch of the "ideal life" or this dream of happiness, then this is what will happen. I advocate that we instead move forward with life step by step, looking at the self realistically.

It is our responsibility to clarify the meaning of our life in terms of our true place of return and to live as if having arrived at our life's ultimate destination. Even though modern-day people devote many years or even decades to acquiring business or technical skills or carrying out academic research, they hate to take a moment to think about their ultimate place of refuge. But when it comes to contemplating one's own final place of return, I can't figure out why so many people fall asleep.

On the surface, our culture is in full bloom. But in my opinion, we haven't advanced one step beyond our primitive and savage past. Even though we fly around in supersonic jets, if we don't examine our place of final refuge, we are nothing more than primitives flying around. Also, in the same vein, we threaten each other with weapons of mass destruction and have completely lost sight of a culture based on seeking our final place of refuge. The Buddha and the ancient Zen ancestors made singular efforts to create a culture based on finding one's ultimate refuge in life and taking refuge in the Three Treasures. They have left this great legacy for us, which I don't want to leave buried in the dust. Rather, I want to create a path to bring the Buddha's teachings to life again for the sake of our current and future generations.

For this reason, I have taken the Kannon-gyo (Avalokiteshvara Sutra), a short Buddhist text, and I wish to share this precious legacy of the Buddhist religion and make it come alive for modern people to appreciate. I will be elated if the reader gains a pure appreciation of the Buddhist religion, either through the practice of chanting *Namu Kanzeon Bosatsu* (I take refuge in the Bodhisattva Kanzeon), or the Pure Land practice of chanting the name of Amida Buddha, the nenbutsu—that is, *Namu Amida Butsu*. Or also Dogen's practice of *shikantaza*, just sitting zazen. I believe that the Kannon-gyo penetrates and unifies these two major streams of Buddhism, pure zazen practice and pure chanting practice.

1. My Personal Connection with the Kannon-gyo

There's a saying in Japan that doctors neglect their own health and Buddhist priests lapse from their faith, and I am certainly one of those priests if you're talking about practicing the old established religion. I've had an iconoclastic tendency since my student days, but before I became a priest, I felt that Buddhist statues were special and mysterious. But, after taking Buddhist vows, I lost that feeling, and now I regard those statues as something like Japanese dolls. Honestly speaking, despite the phrase "truth proceeds from magnificence"—that somehow these icons must have majesty—well, I think that they are nothing more than ornaments. I have come to think of their effect as nothing more than decorative.

One time I attended a sesshin at a nunnery. The abbess tasked me with offering water or tea or flowers morning and evening to the Buddhist statues. I was shocked by how many statues there were—large and small ones, old and new, about twenty or thirty altogether. I was flabbergasted that I had to make an offering to every single one!

Later, in a roundabout way, I mentioned this to my teacher Sawaki Roshi and asked his impression. I said, "Don't you think that these nuns offer flowers and water and take care of these Buddha statues with the same loving care that a girl gives to her dolls?" With a bitter smile, he said, "You're always taking such a cynical point of view!" Well, it appears that I am a habitual cynic.

I'm sure that some people frown when I bandy about these wild points of view. But here what I want to talk about—and what I would like to ask you to listen to—are the words of Kannon Bodhisattva. Knowing this story about me is a prerequisite for understanding my tendency toward iconoclasm and cynicism. So, when it comes to the Buddha statues enshrined in temple halls and in altars in homes, and the ideas of the established conservative religious order, I would like to destroy them and, having eliminated these notions, I want to start thinking about the meaning of Kannon Bosatsu.

Once a monk asked the Chinese Zen master Nanyang Huizhong, "What is the mind of the ancient Buddha?" The master replied, "Fences, walls, tiles and pebbles." According to the master's answer, it is a mistake to think that the Buddha has a special form and emits radiant light and so forth. The Buddha is simply fences, walls, tiles, and pebbles. So, if what Huizhong said is true, my feeling about Buddhist statues does not show a lack of faith in Buddhism.

Yet the Kannon images we see in Buddhist temples and home altars are not Avalokiteshvara. Also, the valuable images of Kannon found in the ancient temples in Nara and Kyoto that we appreciate as fine art are certainly not the bodhisattva incarnate. Since there is no historical person named Kannon, this is nothing more than religion that we should understand as the expression of the life force of our original self.

Please permit me to tell you the story of my personal connection with the Kannon-gyo. In 1944 and 1945, shortly before Japan lost World War II, all Japanese people were suffering through hard times, and I was no exception. Since my teacher, Sawaki Roshi, made it his principle not to have his own temple, my fellow disciples and I had been practicing zazen at Daichuji Temple in Tochigi Prefecture. But then in the summer of 1944 we had to leave to make way for some schoolchildren who had evacuated from Tokyo in order to stay at the temple. Though originally there had been seven or eight of us practitioners, by this point some had left and only three of us remained, now with no place to go. Moreover, in those days, if you weren't already engaged in work directly related to the war effort, you would be conscripted to work in a factory. It was Sawaki

Roshi's and our wish for the three of us to stay together, find some work to do, and continue our zazen practice.

At that time, someone suggested as a joke that we should go deep in the mountains of Shimane Prefecture and work as charcoal makers. It certainly was a wild idea, and I don't hate wild ideas. Since I was born and raised in the big city of Tokyo, I thought that it would be a piece of cake to tend a warm charcoal kiln during the winter in the mountains. I thought that I could probably sit reading a book in front of the kiln. When I look back on it now, it was a hilarious pipe dream.

We received Roshi's permission, and the three of us headed off to the mountains of Shimane Prefecture. To get to this place where our fate had led us, we took a train for about ten hours from Kyoto, finally arriving at a small, out-of-the-way village. Then we took a bus that ran only twice a day, all the way to the end of the line. After that, we walked another five miles to get to a small farmhouse in a glen belonging to a family to whom we had an introduction.

When we arrived, the family showed us where we were going to live and sleep, on the second floor of the farmer's small storage shed. Only half the floor had tatami mats, and there was no electric light. Since there was no kerosene allocated for lamps in those days, we economized by using candles that we appropriated from the local temple, using them as if they were treasures to light our room. The mountainside where we worked was about an hour's walk along a narrow mountain road, alongside a cliff on the sunless north face of the steep mountainside. We could look down into a steep valley in the deep mountains. It was quiet and beautiful scenery.

I had never used a woodsman's saw before, and I had to carry a large heavy axe. When we were guided into the woods, we could scarcely carry the heavy tools as we climbed up and over rocks and balanced on tree roots. We didn't have enough strength either in body or mind to do that work, and for a while the three of us were in a daze. Given that we had finally been able to get permission to evacuate despite severe wartime travel restrictions and had come a great distance from Tokyo to the deep mountains, we had to stay whether we liked it or not. So, I made a desperate effort to somehow get used to the work.

During the Shimane winter you can count the number of days of clear weather on your fingers. We arrived in December, and almost every day a cold north wind dumped snow on the mountains. Shimane Prefecture faces the Sea of Japan, which gets frigid weather fronts coming from Siberia. Since we knew only the climate of warm places in Japan that faced the Pacific Ocean, we were excited by the snow. At first, we thought we could take the day off—hooray! But the locals soon labeled us as lazy. They always worked on days when it snowed—if they took snow days off, there wouldn't be any workdays left.

So, we resolved to live and work with great diligence. We got up while it was still dark, made a breakfast that we ate by candlelight, and then left for work as soon as it was light. All day we used saws and axes to cut down large trees, stripping off branches to make logs that would go into the charcoal kiln. We threw the logs down the valley from midway up the mountain. The mountain slope was very steep, so we were able to heave the logs from the mountain all the way down to the valley floor.

Then we would remove the charcoal we had fired from the kiln, cut it into smaller pieces, and pack it in bags made from rice straw. Also, in those days, we couldn't get proper shoes, so we made our own straw sandals out of thick coarse straw and wore those over our bare feet. As a result, our feet were always raw, cut, and scarred. We didn't have gloves and had to handle the charcoal with our bare hands. When we reached into the kiln between the pieces of charcoal and ash, in a flash we would get burned with blisters all over our hands. Then we'd jump around writhing in pain when the burning charcoal embers stuck on our skin in the spaces between the burns and blisters.

On top of that, food was rationed. We got no food from the government, so we had to consume what little rice we managed to save with great economy. We decided to eat two cups of rice a day per person, dividing that into three meals, making watery rice gruel and drinking it. Our only food besides rice was daikon radishes that we gnawed on raw with a little salt. Eating just made us feel hungrier. If we could have somehow stolen food, that would have been good, but there wasn't any food to steal in the winter in the deep mountains.

We worked all day long, and in the evening, we carried heavy straw bags of charcoal on our backs to the farmhouse. On the way, we had to cross some log bridges that were only two or three narrow logs wide. The bridges were icy, so sometimes we got injured when we slipped and fell into the stream along with our wood-frame backpacks loaded with the heavy straw bags of charcoal. At last, we would manage to cross over the bridges and arrive home. By that time, it was completely dark. Then we prepared our dinner by candlelight, ate it, and immediately went to bed. That was our life that winter.

In the beginning, I often woke in the middle of the night, and the blisters and open sores on my hands hurt. When I moved my body even just a little, my joints cracked so loudly that I wondered if my bones were breaking. It was not easy to get used to that. While I hated my situation, it was out of the question to jump on a train and go back to Tokyo, given that this was toward the end of the war. We spent a dejected, gloomy, and dark winter in those mountains.

One morning we awoke as usual in the dark, and it was snowing. The mountain and valley before us were a total whiteout covered with snow. A bitterly cold wind was blowing hard. Even though I didn't think I was suffering, I certainly was in dark despair. Then when I remembered the work that I would be doing all day long, I started to tense up. If I somehow lost my concentration out there, there was a real danger of falling off the mountain or slipping off one of those bridges, or having my fingers chopped off by an axe—especially in those snowy and icy conditions. As I was preparing breakfast in this tense and despairing state of mind, at some point I became aware that I was unconsciously repeating in my mind *Namu Kanzeon Bosatsu, Namu Kanzeon Bosatsu*—"I take refuge in Avalokiteshvara Bodhisattva," a mantra used to invoke the name of and take refuge in the bodhisattva of compassion.

Even now I don't understand why on earth I suddenly began chanting *Namu Kanzeon Bosatsu*. Looking back, it seems there's no other explanation except that I had had a deep connection with the bodhisattva through exposure in my childhood. On the grounds of my childhood home, from the time of my great-grandfather, there had been a small chapel that enshrined one hundred miniature statues of Kanzeon, representing the temples on the Kannon pilgrimage routes of Saigoku, Chichibu, and Bando. A nun lived there as a caretaker. I heard that my great-grandfather did not like the Pure Land temple that my family belonged to, so in protest he probably built his own chapel and enshrined the Kanzeon images.

The chapel had been dismantled by the time I was born. Instead, there were two chapels on the grounds—until my house burned down during the Great Kanto Earthquake in 1923. One of the chapels was large enough to accommodate three tatami mats, and the other six. On the eighteenth of every month—Kanzeon's day—a group came and sang *goeika* (Buddhist hymns of praise) to Kanzeon. When I was a young boy, I looked forward to these monthly events. My mother had taken three of those statues from the house during the earthquake, and afterward, for as long as my family lived in the house, the group continued to come and sing the songs of praise to Kanzeon. Both my grandmother and mother were pious devotees of Kanzeon Bosatsu as a folk religion. I am told that my mother chanted the Kannon-gyo every day while she was pregnant with me. And later, she continued to chant it every day until she died. She often told me that it was why I eventually became a monk.

Probably due to my childhood experiences, I spontaneously began chanting *Namu Kanzeon Bosatsu*. If I had been a child, I certainly would have called out "Mama!" but instead I said *Namu Kanzeon Bosatsu*. At that time, I felt that there was nowhere else that I could turn to for help.

In any case, in the mountains, preparing breakfast and chanting silently, at some point I began to relax. Although the tension did not dissipate completely, the dark gloominess and stress disappeared. I remember feeling fresh energy within myself and thinking that something mysterious and wonderful had happened.[21]

Even though I had had this connection from my past, up until that day in Shimane I had never thought about the bodhisattva Kannon, and I hadn't had the slightest interest in reading the Kannon-gyo. However, after this experience, I suddenly wanted to read it, and quickly sent a letter to my mother and asked her to send me a copy with Japanese annotations for the Chinese characters. I knew that my mother kept some of the printed copies that my great-grandfather had commissioned for special occasions. I knew that she truly treasured them. After receiving the sutra from my mother, every morning I stuffed it into my pocket as I went to work in the mountains, and I read it whenever we had a short break.

During that period when I lived in that remote area, deep in the mountains of Shimane Prefecture, eking out a living making charcoal, there was no time for zazen. Reading the Kannon-gyo was my sole comfort.

21. According to Okumura Roshi, this is what Uchiyama Roshi means by his expression "opening the hand of thought": spontaneously letting go of our thoughts and feelings while practicing zazen or chanting. Or, as Dogen would say, "Dropping off body and mind."

2. The Sound That Perceives the World

Hearing Freely without Clinging

While living that difficult life in the mountains, I discovered how to appreciate the rather mysterious expressions in the Kannon-gyo. I was reading a Japanese version rendered from the Chinese text. The sutra begins with a question from another bodhisattva, the Bodhisattva of Inexhaustible Intent, who asks the Buddha, "For what reason (what cause and conditions) did Kannon get his name, Perceiver of the World's Sounds?" The Buddha's reply is mysterious. He says,

> Suppose there are immeasurable hundreds, thousands, ten thousand, millions of living beings who are undergoing various trials and suffering. If they hear of this bodhisattva Perceiver of the World's Sounds and wholeheartedly call his name, then at once he will perceive the sound of their voices and they will all gain deliverance from their trials. For this reason, he is called Kanzeon (Perceiver of the World's Sounds).

What is so strange about this answer? Well, usually in order to call a name there needs to be someone who already had that name—that's why we can call someone by their name. I am called Uchiyama-san because a person exists who is called Uchiyama-san. If someone calls me by that name, I respond, "Yes." But in the Kannon-gyo this is not the case. First of all, living beings suffer, and everything starts from when they wholeheartedly, without thinking, call out the name. What name did the first person to call on Kanzeon call out? Well, you simply call out, and Kanzeon perceives the sound, answering "Yes." Living beings will all gain deliverance from their suffering. The Buddha said that when this bodhisattva perceives the cries of the world and responds, he is given the name Kanzeon Bosatsu. This is a strange phenomenon. It is clear that Kannon is not just some wooden or metal representation, and of course Kannon is not a historical person. So, what is Kanzeon?

This is how I interpret the words of the sutra: "When a person is in distress and suffering, and when they call out wholeheartedly, by this action some kind of mysterious power comes into play, and we will immediately gain deliverance from our suffering." This is the process described in the sutra. This process happens because we humans all have an innate ability to employ this inherent power within ourselves, and this is named Kanzeon Bosatsu. If it is correct to understand that Kanzeon is the power that works to free us from suffering when we call out wholeheartedly, then we can relate this to the crucial Soto Zen phrase, "Sanzen (zazen) is dropping off body and mind" or "Dropping off body and mind is zazen" taught to Dogen by his teacher in China, Tiantong Rujing, discussed by Dogen in *Hokyoki*.[22] In Asia since ancient times, we have studied the structure of the self through body and mind during our practice, training, and personal experience. We have been refining practices for a long time based on reciting the name of Amitabha, which is the practice of the Pure Land sect of Buddhism and sitting zazen.

In any case, this experience was the first step that I took in appreciating the Kannon-gyo. After that, for a period of about twenty years I integrated my zazen practice with deepening my appreciation for this

22. Hokyoki (宝慶記), literally "Diary of the Hokkyo Era." This work was found in Dogen's room in draft form at Eiheiji by Ejo Dogen's disciple after his death. It contains a record of conversations that Dogen had in China with his teacher Tiantong Rujing. The work is written in Chinese. For an English translation see Kazuaki Tanahashi, *Enlightenment Unfolds: The Essential Teachings of Zen Master Dogen* (Boston: Shambhala Publications, 1999), 10.

sutra. At some point, I came to the conviction that the name Kanzeon should be read as the Sound that Perceives the World[23] instead of the traditional reading, Perceiver of the World's Sounds. That reading is derived from a treatise on the Kannon-gyo called "The Deep Meaning of Kannon" written by Tiantai Zhiyi (538–97 CE), an important master of the Tiantai sect of Buddhism. Tiantai Zhiyi writes,

> Because Kanzeon Bosatsu thoroughly illuminates the true nature (of reality) and realizes it from beginning to end as a whole, he is called perceiver (the subject of the sentence). So, the sound of the world is the object of the bodhisattva's perceiving.

In other words, Zhiyi interprets Kanzeon to mean "the perceiver of the world's sounds."

However, looking at zazen practice and nenbutsu practice as the main threads of Buddhism, I have come to believe that reading Kanzeon as "the sound that perceives the world" is the best way to exactly express our religious faith and practice. Therefore, we should not think of the zazen practice of the Soto Zen and the nenbutsu practice of the Pure Land sect as incompatible; rather, we must understand them as being one unified Buddhadharma. I believe that we must understand this Buddhadharma to be none other than our own religious life.

23. *Kanzeon* is written 観世音, with the characters for "perceive," "world," and "sound," respectively. Uchiyama Roshi chooses to interpret this as "the sound that perceives the world." According to Uchiyama, Tiantai Zhiyi's rendering—that is, Perceiver of the Sounds of the World—separates subject (perceiver) and object (the sounds of the world). Uchiyama often inverted the epithet—the Sound That Perceives the World—to refer to our practice of chanting without any dualistic separation. Our voice (even if we chant silently) is itself the Kanzeon that perceives (sees) the sounds of the world. Seeing instead of hearing the sound severs the dualistic tie between our sense of hearing and the object of hearing—thus there is no dualistic separation between subject (the one who is chanting) and object (the sounds of the world). Wholeheartedly chanting or calling out Kanzeon's name is the same as when we let go of the hand of thought in zazen, not separating one into two, and not chanting with clinging or attachment.

Zen uses direct expressions to point to the absolute: "not to be grasped," meaning that which cannot be measured with our human intellect; or "no thinking," meaning unknowable by human intellect. At one time the absolute was expressed by words like *God* or *emptiness* or "no permanent (fixed) self." In other words, perceiving the world before any measurement, and with an attitude absent of measurement. According to the Lotus Sutra, "Only among buddhas can the true character of all things be fathomed." Similarly, the Nirvana Sutra says, "Buddha nature can only be known by buddhas."

So, the word *perceiver* in the name Kanzeon is nothing other than this perceiving the world before yardsticks, and with an attitude absent of yardsticks. This is like how a child's mind perceives the world, as in the Bible: "Unless you change and become like little children, you will never enter the kingdom of heaven"; or as it says in the Nirvana Sutra, "the practice of an infant"—that is, bodhisattva practice free from discriminating thoughts, like how an infant behaves naturally without thinking. Before, I used the words "human intellect," but I didn't mean that in the sense of some half-baked adult intellect, but completely polishing it up like the mind of a child.

The *perceiver* part of Kanzeon is the absolute view: it is perceiving from the point of view of having arrived at your life's ultimate destination, having finally returned to a true way of life after having taken refuge in the Buddha, Dharma, and Sangha.

3. The Main Thread of the Buddhadharma

To understand my interpretation of the Kannon-gyo, it is necessary to learn what I mean by "the main threads of the Buddhadharma." My explanation may meander a bit, but please allow me to tell you about my fundamental attitude.

Christ set out to Capernaum on foot. He was accompanied by his twelve disciples, and one of the disciples started talking, asking the question, "Who among us is the worthiest to enter heaven?" Then each disciple thought to himself that if he was lucky, Christ would look back and name and certify him as the worthiest to enter heaven. They all walked along arguing until at long last they finally reached Capernaum. When they reached their lodgings, Christ called the twelve disciples to him and asked them sternly, "What where you are arguing about today?" No one could say anything. Then he told them, "If anyone wants to be first, he must be the very last, and the servant of all." Aren't these words magnificent and profound?

Sometimes in Japan, when some sleepyhead gets certified by a priest as having had an insignificant enlightenment experience, they think that they want to become an important person. These people could never comprehend Christ's profound words. But the question I would like to consider is found in the following passage:

> Christ knew of their deluded minds, and he took a little child and had him stand among them. Taking him in his arms, he said to them, "I tell the truth, unless you change and become like little children,

you will never enter the kingdom of heaven. Therefore, whoever humbles himself like this child is the greatest in the kingdom of heaven."[24]

Christ is saying that if you are the kind of person who wants to be important, this kind of insistent, selfish, self-serving behavior has absolutely nothing to do with entering heaven. Chapter 16 of the Lotus Sutra uses the expression "honest, upright, and gentle," meaning that one must become free from doubts based on personal self-centered ideas. Further, the title of chapter 26 of the Nirvana Sutra can be translated as "child's action," and it describes the innocence of a child.

At the heart of religious faith there is no distinction between East and West. I think we must be like a little child and get down on our knees in supplication with a sincere mind. In order to enter into religion, do we really need to be like a pure and innocent child ?

I am reminded of something Rousseau wrote: "If I had to depict the most heart-breaking stupidity, I would paint a pedant teaching a child the catechism."[25] What I picture, sort of like in a comic book, is a nervous religious maniac explaining a complex doctrinal problem to a child. I can't help but laugh out loud.

The founders of all kinds of so-called religious orders tell their pious yet naive and ignorant followers with fanatical authority that they must "become like a child." Or, they say things like "You won't be saved unless you believe in this god," or "If you don't believe in this religion, you won't find happiness." Believers are told frightening things such as "If you don't follow me your illnesses won't get better," or "If you don't believe this, then your family line will die out." These so-called religions fanatically sell their goods as if at auction. For me, I feel deeply uneasy about religions that are based on mythological explanations like "In the

24. Matthew 18:2–4.

25. Jean-Jacques Rousseau, *Emile, or On Education,* bk. 4.

beginning there was God." Furthermore, when they talk about "curing diseases," I feel that I must criticize these statements as inappropriate. Instead, I must become like a child and also use my critical adult intellect when evaluating these statements.

Actually, most modern people with cool common sense, when they see these fanatical believers in these selfish or mythological religions, they feel sorry for these clowns without becoming clowns themselves. Like me, they adopt a critical, adult frame of mind. At the same time that these extreme fanatics are increasing exponentially, reasonable people categorize religion as the wild ideas of some eccentrics and are simply indifferent to the increasing numbers of fanatical religions. We don't need to buy religions as if they are goods sold at the auction house of these fanatics. Actually, we don't need to even be involved with these auction houses. Being involved with these auction houses is the activity of vulgar people.

In the event that we feel an inner need to express our interest in religion, and we take to heart Christ's message to "become like a child" and actually try and do it, in modern Japan that type of pure spirit of pious believers will be instantly torn apart. In the event that we take some interest in and enter into that dangerous zone called religion, I have thought since my student days that before we become serious believers, we first need to use our adult intellect and employ a critical eye toward religion.

My attitude is as follows: I offer sweeping criticism of and say goodbye to all self-centered, authoritarian religions based in mythology. What's more, I reject not only religions based on myths but also religions based on metaphysics and psychology. I also reject research that analyzes the accuracy of the historical facts surrounding the Buddha or Christ as representing the truth of Buddhism or Christianity. In the final analysis, I also reject the notion that history, bibliographies, linguistics, and so forth are a necessary prerequisite for understanding religion.

I don't believe that religion means that you must take orders from some artificially created religious authority. Since my student days I have felt that all I need to do is to seek the truth of the self, and I resolved not to get involved with any one religion or sect. I started saying that I just wanted to live the life of the self. This was the time when I came upon Shakyamuni Buddha and Dogen Zenji.

In the case of Shakyamuni, although he was influenced by ancient cultural myths, his teaching about life was not based on them. The suffering of the raw life of the self was Shakyamuni's starting point. Through this suffering he taught others that living the life of the self is our final resting place. In verse 160 of the Dhammapada it is said, "The self is the master of the self."[26] Also, Dogen wrote, "To learn the Buddha Way is to learn about the self." Both Shakyamuni Buddha and Dogen were essentially different from standard religious practitioners, and their point of view resonates with how I want to live.

While Dogen Zenji started out with this same attitude, he was also inclined to completely follow in the footsteps of the Buddhist ancestors. Why was that? Dogen explained it in *Shobogenzo Jisho Zanmai* ("Self-Verification Samadhi" as translated by Okumura Roshi): "When following a teacher or a sutra, in all cases, we follow the self. The sutra is nothing other than the sutra of the self; the teacher is nothing other than the teacher of the self."[27] Dogen further explains in the same text that "seeking the true self is completely devoting oneself to the ancestral teachers who sought the true self, and completely devoting oneself to these ancestral teachers is in itself seeking the true self."

In other words, Dogen says that trying for self-verification and self-realization by yourself and thinking that one can't learn Buddhist truth from anyone else is nothing other than acting from a prejudiced,

26. The full verse is "The self is the master of the self. Who else can that master be? With the self fully subdued, one obtains the sublime refuge which is very difficult to achieve." From Harischandra Kaviratna trans., *Dhammapada: Wisdom of the Buddha* (Pasadena, CA: Theosophical University Press, 1980), canto 12, https://www.theosociety.org/pasadena/dhamma/dham12.htm.

27. Unpublished translation by Shohaku Okumura.

egotistic, and heretical point of view. To be precise, one must be completely absorbed in studying and living the truth of the self—and living the truth of the self of the Buddhist ancestors. This is the true meaning of self-verification and self-realization.

Living the truth of the self and insisting on one's own selfish point of view are two different things. When I was suddenly exposed to the views of Shakyamuni Buddha and Dogen, and since I had already decided not to get involved with the type of religion that is sold like goods at an auction house, I completely forgot about Buddhism as being that type of religion and decided to follow Buddhism as taught by these ancestors. It was fortunate that I was able to meet and study with my teacher, Kodo Sawaki Roshi. Sawaki Roshi followed in the same Buddhist stream as Shakyamuni Buddha and Dogen, teaching "To practice zazen is to be intimate with the self. It is the self selfing the self."[28] Having arrived at this point of view in my student days, I then became a Buddhist priest, and I still think that this is indeed what true religion is.

Religions that were based on mythology, metaphysics, psychology and historical research, or the existence of doctrines, creeds, and ecclesiastical authority existed in the past. However, in the times and places these religions flourished, they had little contact with each other, such that each had a monopoly in their era and region. Rousseau also says in *Emile*, "Let a Turkish person, who thinks Christianity so absurd at Constantinople, come to Paris and see what the French think of Mahomet."[29] Nowadays, a Turkish person from Constantinople (Istanbul) can easily travel to Paris and perceive what is happening and what people are thinking. Therefore, Rousseau's observation that the religion that a person believes in is simply a matter of geography is no longer true.

Nowadays, religions appear all together in the marketplace of world religions, and we can compare them freely at any time. However, as we

28. Uchiyama and Okumura, *Zen Teaching of Homeless Kodo*, 25.

29. *Emile*, bk 4.

compare these religions, at some point we can't call them true religions. In fact, we are living in an age when we understand them as simply goods being auctioned off as religions.

It is not at all surprising that many modern people assert, based on a mature scientific point of view, that they don't believe in religion. I myself am a child of this modern era. When I realized that I had no connection with and was indifferent to historical religion, I didn't know what to do with the anguish in my own life. I didn't know where I should turn to unravel this pain—I just held on to it inside myself. When I resolved to pursue a different course, I followed in the path of religion connected to Shakyamuni Buddha and Dogen.

In my view, the main thread of Buddhism is first found when you fix your gaze on the life of the self. You must arrange your entire life around making Buddhism your final resting place, vowing to take refuge in the Three Treasures: the Buddha, the Dharma, and the Sangha. I believe that investigating the life of the self must also be the universal path of humanity, and that universal path must be based on true religion.

When we look at the Buddhist religion, naturally a lot of dust and garbage has adhered to it over time, since it is ancient—but also the purest treasure remains. That treasure is what I have been describing as the main thread of Buddhism. We need to pull this out of the garbage and make it a standard of our practice. In this book, I have taken up the Kannon-gyo and would like to make the appreciation of this sutra nothing other than the appreciation of the main thread of Buddhism.

4. An Unobstructed View of Life and the World

Experiencing Suffering and Agony

After I became a monk, I visited my parents' home only once a year. Likewise, I only set foot in my brother's house once a year. It was during the war, and my brother always kept chickens at his house. Separate from the other chickens was a bantam hen that I heard was called Chibi. This hen was a stray with a great personality and was very skilled at raising her chicks.

Toward the end of the war, my brother was evacuated to the countryside, and he brought Chibi along. In my brother's household of animal lovers, Chibi continued to sit on and incubate batch after batch of her eggs. The eggs hatched and the chickens got big, and they in turn laid eggs. My brother would give the eggs to the farmers, who would give him rice in return. Because of this, during the final days of the war and thereafter, when there were shortages of everything, Chibi was able to help my brother's family food and economic situation. My brother joked to his wife, "Chibi was just like an assistant to you." During the hard times of the evacuation, she worked heroically with my sister-in-law to provide the family with a side business.

I seldom visited my brother's home, and my impression of Chibi is based on little personal experience. But one time when I visited, no one was home, and I happened to see an old copy of a school essay that my brother's daughter Riruko had written. It was titled "The Life of Chibi." Riruko was a high school sophomore at that time, but she had written the essay when she was in sixth grade. Since I hadn't seen Chibi around for a while, I picked up the essay and started reading, as I wondered what had happened to the hen. Here is Riruko's essay.

The Life of Chibi

Chibi was the name of a bantam Chabo hen that we kept at our house. When I was four, we lived in Tokyo's Fujimidai district. It had beautiful scenery with pine trees silhouetted by Mount Fuji in the background. One morning the garden of our house was white, covered with snow, and when my sister told me that there was a dove in the garden, I jumped up and ran outside, startling the bird who jumped up on the roof. We shouted out loudly, "Hey there's a dove, there's a dove!" In those days, we called our mother Mama. In our garden, there was a chicken coop, and just as Mama arrived on the scene, the bird jumped down off the roof and landed just in front of the entrance to the chicken coop. Mama said that it wasn't a dove, but a chicken and she caught it and inquired about it at the neighborhood association. But, since everyone said that it wasn't theirs, we decided to keep it. According to my mother, in those days, many people left dogs behind when they were evacuated during the war, and so there were many packs of stray dogs and they attacked chickens. That was probably how the scared bird got to us. Even at our house before Chibi showed up a pack of about eight dogs made off with our rabbit and a chicken.

When we captured Chibi she was still a chick, all white and very cute. At our house, besides her, we had four large hens, and I still remember that I named one of them Hanako. Because my Mama felt sorry for Chibi, she put her in with Hanako's brood. When we did that there was a commotion, and we discovered that the other chickens had pecked Chibi until her head was completely red with blood. We again felt sorry for her, and my mother put her in a large cage of her own. The peck marks remained, and she was never able to grow new feathers. From then on, she was bald in that spot. She never got very big, but after a while we heard her clucking loudly; she had hatched a little yellow chick. That was the first time I understood the word *Chabo*, a variety of domestic bantam chicken native to Japan. We gave her the name Chibi (Shorty).

As the war worsened, we too were evacuated. We took both Hanako and Chibi with us to the countryside. We came here to a small village in Saitama Prefecture in March when I was five years old. In April, my older sister entered the village grammar school. There were rice fields and vegetable gardens. Since Chibi was always calm and never made mischief, we let her roam free in the fields. At night, we put her in an apple box to sleep by herself. After Chibi went in and went to sleep, it was always my chore to put the lid on top of her box.

She got completely used to it, never ran away, and was always by our side. Chibi was always by herself and didn't have any friends, so I guess that she was lonely. If my mother was in the kitchen, Chibi was there; if my mother went out to the field, Chibi always trailed behind her eating insects. When the weather got warmer, Chibi would cluck while starting to make a nest. My mother got six eggs from the neighbors and put them in with Chibi who happily sat on the eggs. One morning Mama said that chicks were hatched, so when we quietly went to see, the cute bright yellow chicks stuck their heads out from under Chibi's wings. Since it was the first time that chicks hatched at our house, my mother didn't know what to do, so she quickly took them out of the nest, but Chibi was really good at raising chicks. At first, she stayed near the nest and didn't go far. Then she would stand a little and then squat down and keep the chicks close to her body and rest.

Every day she would take the chicks a bit farther from the nest. When she wanted to eat, she would peck at our toenails. I was impressed by Chibi and thought that she was extraordinary. Because the chicks were gamecocks, they soon got taller than her. Since gamecocks are fighters, they soon began puffing up their necks and fighting among themselves.

When this happened, Chibi's face would turn red and she would start pecking the roosters that were bigger than her to keep them in line.

After a while, Chibi didn't call the other chicks when she found food, and she started playing by herself again. When she started to play by herself, she started to lay eggs. Because Chibi's eggs were very small and beautiful, once right after she had laid an egg, I put it in my mouth. When I did that, my older sister made fun of me saying, "She put the egg that just came out of the chicken's rear in her mouth," and that made me realize what I did, and I still remember quickly spitting out the egg.

When I entered grammar school, we borrowed a handsome rooster from a nearby farm and we let them stay together for a time. When chicks were born, both Chibi and the rooster clucked, and we fed them. We were really glad that Chibi was so excellent at incubating the chicks.

In the spring when I entered second grade, when Chibi was sitting on four Plymouth chicks, Mama got thirty Leghorn chicks from Tochigi Prefecture and put them together in Chibi's nest one night. So Chibi's brood suddenly got very large. She worked hard and was always busy making sure the chicks were fed. We buried some burning charcoal in the ashes of our *irori*[30] and put the cage with Chibi and the chicks on top of it to keep them warm. Since the chicks were warm, they spread out in the box and slept.

When it was time for bed, Chibi would go right to the chicks and spread her wings as wide as she could and get the chicks near her body. There were more than thirty chicks, and since Chibi thought she would get them close to her under her wings she looked like a tent.

I think that this was when Chibi seemed the most healthy and alive. In any case, all the many chickens at our house were raised by this small bantam hen: Shamos, Plymouth, and White Leghorns—all larger than her—but when Chibi came near them, they would all run away in fear.

30. A kind of sunken hearth formerly common in Japanese country homes.

After a few years, when Chibi got older and started losing strength, the other chickens started picking on her. When I was in fourth grade, Chibi gradually got weaker and was mostly unable to walk. She would spend the day sitting and not moving. We felt so sorry for her, so we let her sleep in our kitchen at night.

One day, my mother put Chibi in the sun out on our veranda, leaving the shoji doors open slightly. Mama said that she heard Chibi clucking loudly, but since she was always doing that, my mother didn't think anything of it. But when she no longer heard the clucking, she went out to look. She didn't see Chibi, but instead she saw a brown dog slinking away in the distance. At the same time, one of our neighbors was on his way to our house when he saw a brown dog with something white in its mouth near our neighborhood Shinto shrine. That was the end of Chibi.

When I finished reading this composition I was at a loss for words. While alive, all living things shoulder a heavy burden. I felt that is the condition of our lives, and I was grief-stricken and disconsolate. When we view each other's lives, maybe it's because we're too close to one another, but rather than seeing the entire unobstructed view of our lives we see only partial views: our work life, or our daily routines, or our love life, our hatreds, our conflicts, our joyful times, our sad times; these small parts loom large in front of our eyes, but we aren't often able to see an unobstructed view of our life as a whole. But I felt that this child, Riruko, was able to capture the life of this hen, in a moment of time in her eye, and describe the burden of all living creatures giving us an unobstructed view of our helpless lives.

An Unobstructed View of Our Life

There was a time when Chibi was trying desperately to survive.
But by chance she was able to find a safe place to live.

Then without even thinking about it she had the best of times
every day.
In time, she met a husband.
She worked, she worked feverishly.
Seems like she was born only to work.
She put her complete effort into the work of raising her chicks,
But when they were grown, they began to move away and turned
their backs on her.
She then desperately tried to reassert her authority over the
chicks and guide them.
But at some point, old age began to overtake her, and she began
to weaken and decline.
Her guidance was ignored, and conversely the chicks began to
peck at her and drive her away.
In the blink of an eye, she faced old age alone.
Without even having time to reflect on what her purpose was
in life,
death appeared, and with maybe two or three clucks her life came
to an end.
This is the unobstructed view of life that we see here and there all
around us.
A bottomless sadness.

For me, just one of the countless beings whose life appears and floats away, religion is nothing more than asking myself what was, is, and should be my reason for existence? I believe this is the question that we need to concern ourselves with.

5. The Religious Meaning of Suffering in the World

Looking at the outward structure of the entire Kannon-gyo, we see that it is comprised of two sections: prose and verse. The prose section is also more or less divided into two question-and-answer sections. This structure is illustrated in the following diagram created by Master Tiantai Zhiyi (538–97), the fourth ancestor of the Chinese Tiantai sect. This diagram appears in his work *Guanyin Yishu*, and I will use it as a framework for my discussion.

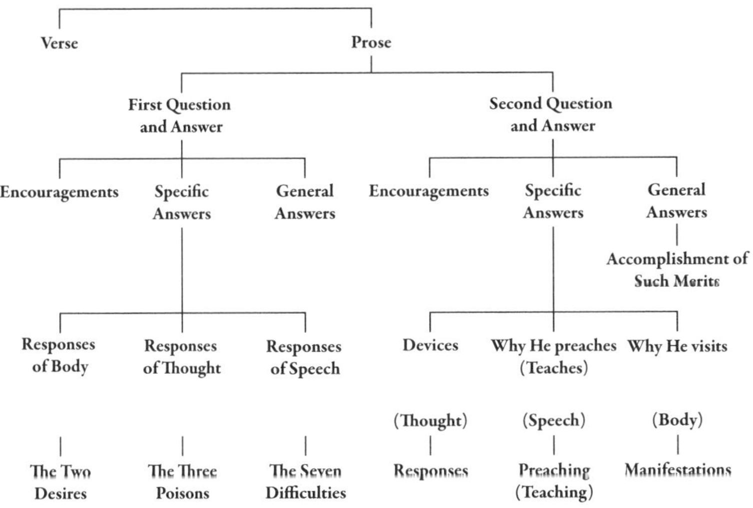

What kind of question opens the sutra? The sutra starts with the Bodhisattva of Inexhaustible Intent facing the Buddha and asking, "For what reason does the Perceiver of the Cries of the World Bodhisattva have the name Perceiver of the Cries of the World?" To answer this, the Buddha said,

> Good son! If there were countless hundreds of thousands of billions of living beings experiencing suffering and agony who heard of Perceiver of the Cries of the World Bodhisattva, and wholeheartedly called his name, Perceiver of the Cries of the World Bodhisattva would immediately hear their cries, and all of them would be freed.

This is the first question and answer. Next, is the "specific answer" section, which gives a more detailed answer:

> "If anyone who embraces the name of Regarder of the Cries of the World Bodhisattva [Kannon] falls into a great fire, the fire will not burn that person, due to the divine authority and power of that bodhisattva. If anyone, carried away by a flood, calls his name, that person will immediately reach some shallows. If there are hundreds of thousands of billions of beings who, in search of gold, silver, lapis lazuli, seashell, agate, coral, amber, pearls, and other treasures, go out to sea and have their ships blown off course by a fierce wind to the land of the ogre demons, and if among them there is even a single person who calls the name of Regarder of the Cries of the World Bodhisattva, all those people will be saved from difficulties caused by the ogres. This is why the bodhisattva is named Regarder of the Cries of the World.
>
> "Or if someone faced with immediate attack calls the name of Regarder of the Cries of the World Bodhisattva, the swords and clubs of the attackers will instantly break into pieces and they will be freed from the danger.
>
> "Even if the three-thousand great thousandfold world were full of satyrs and ogres seeking to torment people, these evil spirits, hearing the people call the name of Regarder of the Cries of the

World Bodhisattva, with their wicked eyes they would not even be able to see them, much less hurt them.

"If, moreover, someone, guilty or not guilty, is captured and put in stocks or manacles and chains, and they call the name of Regarder of the Cries of the World Bodhisattva, their bonds will be broken, and they will be freed.

"Suppose a three-thousand great thousandfold world were full of vengeful thieves, and a caravan leader was guiding a group of merchants carrying costly treasures over a dangerous road. If just one among the merchants speaks out, saying: 'Good sons, do not be afraid. Wholeheartedly call the name of Regarder of the Cries of the World Bodhisattva, for this bodhisattva is able to give courage to all the living. If you invoke this bodhisattva's name, you will be freed from these vengeful thieves.' Hearing this, if all the traders together with one voice cry out, 'Praise to Regarder of the Cries of the World Bodhisattva,' by calling that name they will be freed from the danger."[31]

The next paragraph describes how, by constantly keeping your mind on and venerating Kannon, you separate yourself from the three poisons of lust, anger, and ignorance. This is called "responses of thought"—that is, liberation from the three poisons.

And the paragraph following that says that if you pray to Kannon and offer alms and obeisance, you will have a fine child. This is called "responses of body."

The sutra gives these three conditions—that is, calling out to Kannon, abstaining from the three poisons, and offering alms and obeisance—and then gets around to recommendations to believe in and maintain one's practice—specifically, receiving and holding fast to faith in the Three Treasures: Buddha, Dharma, and Sangha.

31. Reeves, Lotus Sutra, 371–72.

I suggest that everyone read the translation of the Kannon-gyo for themselves.[32] From the very beginning until the end of the sutra, the virtue of Kannon Bosatsu consists of a list of benefits. However, a criticism would be that it sounds like some exaggerated advertisement for medicine, or the kind of miraculous cures promised by some new Japanese religions, which I think we should reject as being ridiculous.

Considering the first answer in the above quotation, it says that when we are undergoing trials and suffering in this world, if we wholeheartedly call out the name Kannon (or Kanzeon), we will be instantly delivered from our problems. Naturally, we would then interpret this to mean, "When we are sick, if we take this medicine then we will be immediately cured" or "When we experience an unfortunate calamity, if we pray to this god (or goddess) then our luck will instantly change."

The quotation continues, and we read that even if we fall into a big fire, we will not be burned, or if we are washed away in a great flood and we're floating in the water, we will immediately find ourselves in a shallow place if we call out the name of the bodhisattva. So then, could you say that someone who holds fast to the name of Kanzeon Bosatsu will not be burned even if she is in the middle of a conflagration caused by an atomic bomb? Or, if you owe a lot of taxes and you call on Kanzeon, then you won't have to pay?

At this point, we need to be careful to understand this from the point of view of the Kannon-gyo. It is not correct to cut this sutra out from the rest of the Lotus Sutra and read the words literally as a standalone work. The Kannon-gyo must be read as part of the complete Lotus Sutra, with the Buddhist teachings as the background and foundation of our lives. If we don't take this foundation into account, and only read the words

32. See appendix 1.

literally, then not only the Kannon-gyo but the entire Lotus Sutra would become just some utilitarian new religion[33] mumbo jumbo.

Among the Buddhist scriptures, the Lotus Sutra, which expounds the purity of the highest Buddhadharma—that is, the teachings of the Buddha—is also said to cure illness. When the Lotus Sutra is used as a source for fanatical sorcery, it is because its words are taken literally. However, since ancient times, the Lotus Sutra has been called the king of the Buddhist canon. The fact that the Kannon-gyo is regarded as one of the four most important chapters in the Lotus Sutra is not because it is read in some sort of superficial, literal way. Rather it is always considered in connection with its deep Buddhist background. Reading the sutra from the standpoint of the foundation of our lives, how does the meaning of the Kannon-gyo change? I will carefully consider this question.

I earlier said that the general answers section of the sutra reads like an exaggerated advertisement for medicines, or a list of over-the-top claims made by one of the Japanese new religions. Let's try an experiment and look at such statements and their implied opposites:

"When I am ill, if I take this medicine, then I will recover." The opposite would be, "When I am not ill, then I don't need to take this medicine." Or, "When I am ill, if I don't take this medicine, then I will not get better."

"When I experience an unfortunate calamity, if I pray to this god, then good fortune will follow." The opposite would be, "If I don't experience an unfortunate calamity, then I do not need to pray." Or, "If I do not pray to this god, then I will not have good fortune."

In "if-then" sentences like these, we can immediately postulate the opposite condition. When we see if-then statements such as "If I take this medicine then I will recover" or "If I believe in this god then I will have

33. "New religions" are those religions founded in Japan since the middle of the nineteenth century. There are many new religions, but most are influenced by older traditions, including Shintoism, Buddhism, Hinduism, and Christianity. Uchiyama felt that adherents of these religions were sometimes fanatical in their beliefs.

good fortune," we are lured in by this kind of bait, and we are persuaded to accept these seemingly sensible and practical arguments.

In the case of an ad for medicine, that might be okay, but in the case of finding truth in the sphere of religious belief, that is when it comes to the Buddha or God, is it really okay to be persuaded by what amounts to a mere advertisement for cure-alls?

Of course, we must use our adult common sense here. How should we understand the Kannon-gyo? We might try to read the words as the standard if-then statements above. "Suppose there are hundreds, thousands, ten thousands, millions of living beings who are undergoing trials and sufferings"—but what we should concern ourselves with here is the word *sufferings*. What exactly does suffering mean? Even though we recognize it, I think that we need to appreciate this word on a deeper level. Perhaps it is a kind of word with such deep meaning that our definitions are inexhaustible.

We usually understand suffering to mean not having any money, getting sick, being oppressed by someone, being in despair, experiencing unrequited love, being unlucky, and so on. With this understanding of suffering, we feel we are being attacked. Suffering is something that comes from the outside, and it is separate from a complete view of the totality of our lives as a whole.

In my case also, I was motivated to read the Kannon-gyo because I was miserable and experiencing just that kind of suffering. When I started to chant *Namu Kanzeon Bosatsu*, I was calling on a deity when I was in distress. As I described in chapter 1, I started reading the Kannon-gyo because of the physical suffering I was experiencing while working as a charcoal maker in the deep mountains of Shimane Prefecture toward the end of the war. Feeling a dark hopelessness, I unconsciously began to call out *Namu Kanzeon Bosatsu*. And then I had the personal experience of somehow being consoled and comforted. I then wanted to know the Kannon-gyo better and read it day and night. Even so, I had a sensible, commonsense mindset, so I could not just say to myself, "When

I encounter suffering, if I call the name of Kanzeon Bosatsu then I will be freed from my suffering." Nor could I feel intoxicated by the phrase or become fanatical about it. On the contrary, having had this unexpected and rather mysterious experience, I began to ponder the meaning of the phrase *Namu Kanzeon Bosatsu*. My speculation about the meaning of my life and my commitment to Buddhism and my zazen practice all started at that time. After about ten years of living with the question, I was able to make some progress in solving the riddle. That was when I came to realize that the meaning of this word *suffering* must be understood from the vantage point of an unobstructed view of the totality of our life.

Without such a vantage point, the meaning of *suffering* becomes subjective. I am reminded of the Japanese proverb, "Travel is troublesome and hard." Of course, travel in olden times was surely difficult! Nowadays air travel is portrayed as pleasant. We think of it as sightseeing instead of just travel. Or think about the era when "old women were abandoned in the mountains."[34] Without a doubt, to be an elderly person in those days must have been a lonely type of suffering. However, with national health insurance and social programs, and with the appearance of nursing homes for the elderly, the meaning of suffering for the elderly has certainly changed. Things that once seemed difficult and full of suffering can change to become easy or even pleasant. Before long, I'm sure we will see ads for such things as "a comfortable hospital life," or "the fun life of the pauper class," or "the wholesome prison life." We all hope that our lives become more comfortable and secure, but should we wish for this in the realm of religion? I think absolutely not! Instead, we expect to

34. *Ubasuteyama*, literally "the mountain where old women or elderly parents are abandoned," also called *oyasute*. "Abandoning a parent" refers to the custom allegedly performed in Japan in the distant past, whereby an infirm or elderly relative was carried to a mountain or some other remote, desolate place, and left there to die, either by dehydration, starvation, or exposure, as a form of euthanasia. The practice was allegedly most common during times of drought and famine and was sometimes mandated by feudal officials.

see these changes emerging from science, economics, politics, or society as a whole. With advances in science and improvements in society, then naturally this type of limited, incidental suffering can be ameliorated—but it is not real suffering in the religious sense.

No matter how much science, society, or the economy progresses, as long as we are human beings we cannot avoid suffering from hopelessness and despair. All living beings without exception must inevitably suffer when we contemplate our lives from an unobstructed point of view that considers our lives as a whole. This is without a doubt the true suffering that religion should address.

As I said before, since we are so close to the events in our lives, we tend to see our lives through the lens of our work, romances, hatreds, and conflicts. These limited and fractured views blind us and prevent us from looking deeply into our lives. So perhaps we should say that our inability to perceive or think about our lives without these obstructions is the true meaning of suffering.

When anyone uses the expression "an unobstructed view of life" incorrectly, I feel that they are always turning their eyes away from true suffering. Just like a pig brought to the slaughterhouse who laps the blood of its slaughtered fellows, we do not view our lives comprehensively. We think only about what is right in front of us, and so we chase a narrow view of our lives. We lose all hope and can only murmur *Namu Kanzeon Bosatsu*.

In any case, when we look at suffering from the point of view of true religion, hidden in the words of the Kannon-gyo—"Suppose there are innumerable human beings who are undergoing every kind of suffering"—we find many more meanings of *suffering*. Remember that the bodhisattva who asks the Buddha about Kanzeon's name is the Bodhisattva of Inexhaustible Intent. So, the meaning of our existence must be appreciated as inexhaustible suffering.

Let's look again at the words from the sutra: "Suppose there are innumerable human beings who are undergoing every kind of suffering." The word *suppose* makes it a conditional sentence, but actually this is not a hypothetical statement; it is instead an absolute statement of fact. Hidden in this seemingly conditional sentence is the fact that our lives are continually soaked in suffering. When we are suffering, we have no choice but to take refuge in the Bodhisattva Kannon. Even though I do not perceive it due to my suffering, I single-mindedly and wholeheartedly chant the name.

Suffering is not something that attacks me only occasionally. No, my life is permeated by suffering. But, drowning in this suffering, I am unable to perceive the truth. I fight with people; I lust and kill. That must be what true suffering is. When I contemplate this, I must call out with a voice as if in grief to vent my despair. But we shouldn't use this wholeheartedly calling out *Namu Kanzeon Bosatsu* just to escape from or give expression to our suffering. Whether we think we are suffering or not, we must wholeheartedly call out[35] day and night as an ongoing religious practice.

35. For Uchyama, "wholeheartedly calling out" or chanting *Namu Kanzeon Bosatsu* or the Pure Land nenbutsu (*Namu Amida Butsu*) is the same as opening the hand of thought in zazen. Please see his book *Opening the Hand of Thought* for a full explanation.

6. Resolving Problems with Money versus Emancipation through Religion

In the preceding chapter I wrote about the meaning of suffering from a religious standpoint. In this chapter I would like to go a step further and contrast religious emancipation with trying to use money to resolve suffering.

The eminent monk and arhat Binzuru (Skt: Pindola-Bharadvaja) comes to mind. His statue is often seen on the verandas of Buddhist temples with a red bib around his neck. There is a sutra that describes a Dharma teaching that Binzuru gave to King Udayana.[36]

King Udayana was the king of Kaushambi in northern India. He was a wise king and a brave and skillful warrior. Since he governed skillfully, his kingdom flourished. He took pride in his country's wealth and power. The arhat Binzuru was originally the son of a minister in this country and a childhood playmate and friend of the king.

But when he grew up, Binzuru left home, was ordained as a priest, and practiced as a disciple of the Buddha attaining the way. After some time as a wandering monk, at one point he came back to Kaushambi, the place of his birth, begged for alms, and sat zazen in the forest. From time to time people saw him and reported this to King Udayana.

One day the king was carried in a palanquin to meet Binzuru. When he saw him, he said, "Your ancestors were ministers for my country, and you

36. The Sutra Spoken by Pindola Bharadvaja for King Udayana.

and I have known each other and been friends for a long time. I would like to speak with you and ask you some questions. You have given up all the worldly pleasures that make life worth living, throwing away the pleasures of the flesh, and you live a lonely life by yourself in the forest. What in the world is so pleasurable that you live like this?" The arhat answered the king's question in this way: "Everything in the world is impermanent and uncertain. Living life based on this uncertainty has no value. Rather we should let go of attachments, leave home, go forth into the mountains, and wholeheartedly cultivate the Way, thus transcending the flow of life and death. That is exactly like a bird in flight who escapes from a net and soars into the limitless sky. As a monk, I have no sorrows. That is emancipation."

Hearing these words, the king felt comfortable speaking with an old childhood friend. He then said, "At this time I have conquered and subjugated other countries, and virtuous prosperity shines down like sunlight on me. I wear a heavenly crown on my head and am adorned with grand clothes, and I am attended on my right and left by beautiful women of noble birth—but you live a lonely life. Are you not jealous of me? "

"Why in the world would I be jealous of you?" answered Binzuru arhat clearly. But the king could not understand his answer, so he asked him again, "Why do you not envy me?" The arhat answered, "King, because I am emancipated from evil passions—that is, carnal desires—I do not seek the beauty of heavenly women or any woman. Why would someone who sees clearly be jealous of someone who is unable to see? Why would a healthy person be jealous of one who is ill? Why would a free person be jealous of a convict? Why would a wealthy person envy someone who is in great poverty? Why would an aristocrat be envious of a manservant? Why would a sage be jealous of a dunce?"

Ah, the conversation has become serious. The king, who has power, wealth, luxury, and keeps company with beautiful women, thinks that this beggar monk who lives in the forest doing zazen must be lonely and must envy the king. But when the king expresses pity for Binzuru, the king instead finds himself compared to a pauper, one who is enslaved, a prisoner, or someone who is infirm. Since Binzuru was an old friend of the king, when the king asked a gentle question to the arhat, he must have felt that Binzuru's answer gave him a glimpse of an unexpected world.

This sutra continues, but what I want to focus on is this issue of Binzuru not being envious of the king. Why isn't this poor beggar monk, who does zazen by himself in the forest, even a little bit jealous of the wealth and power of the king? Some might say that what Binzuru said is just sour grapes. If we don't clarify this matter of money and wealth for ourselves, even if we walk on the path of Buddhist practice, we will waver. However, if we always, all of us together, contemplate this, I feel that we must use Binzuru's example and always be determined and unwavering on this point as we engage in Buddhist practice.

What we usually call suffering is often actually a problem that we think we could take care of if only we had enough money. For example, if one finds that married life has become boring and uninspiring, it can often seem to be because there is not enough money—perhaps the couple is too poor even to get a divorce. However, if at this point there is plenty of money, it is often the case that things get resolved quickly.

Even when we suffer in relationships with coworkers, if you are rich, try throwing plenty of money around in their direction and see what happens. I'm sure that there won't be many people still upset after getting some money or a valuable gift from you, and you will be in the midst of smiling faces and bad feelings will be smoothed over.

When you are ill, and you think about how your family will get by with all the medical expenses, it can be hard. But if money is no object, when you are admitted to a hospital that is like a hotel and you're taken care of so you can recuperate in style, then the suffering caused by your illness is a lot easier to bear. And how about old age? You might say that old age can't be solved by money. But if you have all kinds of money, you might be able to attract a young partner and feel like you have regained your youth.

Everyone in the world thinks that money is more important than anything, so they suffer and toil their entire lives to acquire wealth. Using money to run away from suffering might often seem to work. If all problems can be resolved with cash, then we have to say that there is no need for religion in the world. So-called religions that teach that to make money you need to believe in God or Buddha are worthless, and the reason is clear. There are problems in this world that can't be resolved by wealth, and so more than having faith for the purpose of making money, we must have belief in truth. There must be a religion based on truth. Suffering that we take care of with lots of money is not true suffering—we must call it simply a lack of money. True suffering in our lives cannot be resolved even though we may be wealthy.

What is this suffering that can't be resolved with money? Even if the various fields of science, economics, and politics advance, I'm talking about the kinds of suffering that can't be touched by wealth, technology, and organization. During our lifetimes, we can resolve certain specific difficulties with money, but no matter how much money or power we have, we are nothing but ordinary mortals. Each person during their entire life must bear the burden of unresolved suffering. Or, putting it another way, if I am part of a powerful business conglomerate, or a dictator, I might have an ingrained habit of using only wealth and power to make things right, but as a lone person I might be completely at a loss as to what to do.

And if we're not wealthy, then we think "Ah, if I only had money." And, realizing that we don't have the funds, we sigh and lament, "No one is as miserable as me."

The other day, someone who had endured the anguish of attempting suicide many times came to see me. They told me about all their problems from one to ten. During this conversation, I discovered that they tended not to think of things from another person's point of view at all and were unwilling or unable to try to change their thinking. This person was not at all embarrassed to share their problems with me, and I was intrigued by the fact that their thoughts centered only around themselves and their personal problems. Given their situation, I thought that it might be good for them to try to do something about themselves, but the more this person engaged in self-pity, and the more caught up in their own suffering and personal problems they became, the more deeply confused they got and didn't know what to do. I found it strange that everything became just their grumblings. In this world, for people who believe they bear all suffering alone, their main problem is that they haven't resolved the reality of their own lives, and the depth of their suffering is in direct proportion to the depth of self-pity.

Therefore, what we tend to label "suffering" is a type of suffering that can be resolved with money. Essential suffering, which cannot be resolved by money, lies deeply concealed within us. If we combine the thought of the superficial suffering of having no money with our essential suffering, then our lives are in a constant state of turmoil. So then in this way we as human beings layer problems like having no money over this deeper layer of existential suffering. But speaking from the point of view of religion, even when we have funds to throw money at our suffering and ameliorate some of our problems, we cannot call this gaining deliverance from suffering.

Even if we temporarily solve some external problems, we haven't put to rest the fundamental problem of our deepest suffering, and at some point, this suffering will resurface. However, if we have resolved our fundamental suffering, even if we reach the depths of poverty, we can say we have been delivered from suffering. If you resolve the essential question of who your true self is, then being broke is just being broke, because having no money can't be called true suffering. We need to see this clearly and then take another look at the exchange between King Udayana and the arhat Binzuru.

King Udayana had already said, "Virtuous prosperity shines down like sunlight on me," so he should have been able to resolve all his suffering through wealth and power. But looking at things through the eyes of

Binzuru, from the perspective of religion, we see that Udayana hasn't resolved the question of his true self—and as long as he has not done that, he is a suffering being who is nothing other than someone who is unable to see, someone who is ill, a convict, or an enslaved person. Binzuru is someone who has already resolved the essential suffering that is at the deepest layer. Again, being broke is simply being broke and not really suffering, so Binzuru, despite having no money, was not jealous of the king.

The calculus is different for suffering that can be resolved by money versus the deliverance from fundamental existential suffering. When we consider suffering as a religious problem, we need to separate it entirely from the problem of a lack of funds. As it says in the Bible, "You cannot serve both God and Caesar."

7. God's Yardstick versus Our Human Yardstick

Here is a letter someone wrote to me:

> The other day I had the privilege of reading your "Consolation of Religion." After reading it just once, I felt like a cloud was lifted from my mind. For the past five years I have suffered from Pott's disease (tuberculosis of the spine) and have spent day after day recuperating and lying on my back, not allowed to get out of bed. You can imagine the agitation I have felt during my recuperation. Based on the recommendation of one of my fellow patients, I came to know about the Bible and have visited occasionally with a pastor. But your kind words are easier to understand, and I am very grateful for your explanations and have reread your piece many times. Still, there is something that I can't understand. In your writing titled "Prayer" you quote the commandment from the Bible, "Do not lie"—that is, don't tell a lie, always tell the truth. Then you go on to say that you think that if we tell each other the honest truth and expose all our truly ugly thoughts, there will be serious consequences. So rather than being totally honest and revealing our ugly thoughts, you say you think it is better to keep quiet and perjure ourselves.
>
> Please forgive me for saying this, but I am sorry to say that I am uncomfortable regarding this point about lying. Up until now I have not had painful or sad experiences. Everyone I have met has been a good person. However, these days I have come to know the reverse side of people and I am completely baffled. People who get along

well in society say that lying is kind of a lubricating oil between people. But when the person they are talking to leaves, they stick out their tongue at them behind their back, and when they flatter a person, the person being flattered feels good, but the flatterer says things freely that must put a stain on their conscience. But I try to keep true to myself and maintain a high standard and try my best not to tell even small lies. I'm afraid that if I start perjuring myself by freely telling lies to grease relations with people, that it would soon become a bad habit.

Previously, the abbot of Ryutakuji Temple, Yamamoto Genpo Roshi, said in a morning radio talk, "Zen is living a life without lies," and "white things appear white," but when it comes to people, isn't it too simplistic to just say white things appear white? So temporarily repressing one's own constantly recurring ugly and evil thoughts and filtering them, and skillfully using lies when expedient—doesn't this mean wisdom is lies that become truth? Many people run with this notion, and I find that sometimes I have begun to hate such shallow people, and I find myself bothered by the fact that I have selfish feelings and would rather be alone. I'm sorry to intrude on your time with this letter but hope that you can explain this matter to me.

I replied like this:

I sincerely sympathize with you regarding your long convalescence. However, I think that you are enduring trying times and I pray that, while you will fight this illness with an indomitable spirit, you use this time to live the reality of your life. In any case, regarding your question, I would like to ask you to allow me to answer it honestly and frankly.

We often use the words *truth* and *lie*, but what we call truth is actually just a result of our habits. That is because embedded in words are two meanings: actual fact and truth. I'm not at all saying that I approve of telling lies, but I would like to emphasize the fact that "telling the truth" is often fake. In my experience, people who think they are telling the truth are mostly called "good people," but when they stand before God, are they in reality good people? In the Bible it says there is "no good person, not even one." No matter how much we assume that we are being righteous, we mustn't forget that before God we are nothing more than sinners. To be more precise, when we say something that comes unfiltered from our minds or hearts, we think that we are speaking the truth, but since the words come from the hearts of us sinners, those words must reflect sinful thoughts. By actually speaking these sinful thoughts, we think that we are speaking truthfully, but in fact we are piling up our arrogance. Comparing this to God's truth, aren't we just adding additional layers of sin?

In reality, when we encounter good people who arrogantly think in their heart that they are speaking and acting truthfully, we tend to judge them poorly. We measure what we think is the truth with our own ruler, and when we clumsily attempt to transpose God's truth with ours, then in God's name we judge and condemn and do nothing but fight and kill others.

But this is not true Christian teaching. When we stand before the reality of God, rather than condemning others, we need to reflect with modest humility on the fact that we are only sinners, and with a repentant and prayerful heart we forgive and love others with our entire being. We must try to live a truly Christian life. When we as mere mortals try to transpose our yardstick (that is, our own thoughts and values) onto God's yardstick (that is, love and forgiveness) we create confusion. We use the word *truth*, but we are substituting the sinner's thoughts for God's truth. If we forgive or love someone and then arrogantly announce our forgiveness and love, it is no substitute for God's love. Before God's yardstick, we must always remember the limits of our love, which always leaves something wanting compared to God's love, and we must remain humble.

However insignificant our actions may be, when we walk God's path, I pray that we fully use whatever abilities we have. For example, wouldn't it be good if even you, confined to your bed, adopted a kind heart and forgave, appreciated, comforted, and showed love to your fellow patients and the nursing staff around you? You could always engage those around you with a gentle smile, couldn't you? And because of your bright smile they would be consoled and be brave and feel joy and hope. Don't you think you would ignite the light of love for them? If you do this when you are bedridden, just as you are, you would be working for the sake of God's greater glory, and you would also be spreading his warm love. From the point of view of our usual human yardstick, a sick person lying in bed cannot perform any work, but in the world of religion this is not the case. For example, even a person lying in bed has a mission and must reveal God's glory, and their life also has an endless effect.

Regarding this point, religion is not a measurement taken with a human yardstick, but rather a measurement that God takes in his world with his yardstick. We should never let ourselves forget this.

So, does religion apply to this world as measured by God's yardstick? In the Bible, it is written, "Be concerned above everything else with the kingdom of God and with what he requires of you, and he will provide you with all these other things."[37] It doesn't say that you should seek the justice of the kingdom of man. Again, there is the Bible verse, "It is only our own spirit within us that knows all about us; in the same way, only God's Spirit knows all about God."[38] This is exactly the same meaning as the verse from chapter 2 of the Lotus Sutra, "Skillful

37. Matthew 6:33.

38. 1 Corinthians 2:11.

Means": "Only among buddhas can the true character of all things be fathomed."[39] Similarly, the Nirvana Sutra says, "The Buddha Nature as such can only be known by the Buddha alone and is not within the reach of sravakas and pratyekabuddhas"[40]

These things may be difficult for the average person to understand, but they are especially important to true religion. At the same time, it is human nature that so-called new religions, which are based on fulfilling human desires, are probably much more easily understood.

A common expression is, "It takes a thief to know a thief." In the same way, it goes without saying that God's path should be measured using only God's yardstick. If we measure with our human yardstick, even if we use the word *truth*, as I said before, the words of God's truth will be obscured. Though the reality of God is love, when humans use the word *truth*, they hide in the shadows of that word and thrust accusations and judgments in people's faces. Similarly, when people use the words *love*, *atonement*, *belief*, *repentance*, *prayer*, and so on, as long as they measure using a human yardstick, I believe that these words have nothing to do with God's word. "For God in his wisdom made it impossible for people to know him by means of their own wisdom."[41]

Since there is no way to convert from God's yardstick to a human yardstick, we are completely unable to understand God's yardstick. "What no one ever saw or heard, what no one ever thought could happen is the very thing God prepared for those who love him."[42] When it comes to true religion, for us mere mortals, we are unable to scale this barrier that towers above us.

Basing our thinking on conditioned human wisdom, the path to God's

39. Gene Reeves, trans., "Skillfull Means," chapter 2 in *The Lotus Sutra: A Contemporary Translation of a Buddhist Classic* (Somerville, MA: Wisdom Publications, 2008), 76.

40. Kosho Yamamoto and Tony Page, trans., *The Nirvana Sutra: A Translation of the Dharmakshema's Northern Version*, v. 460, (pub. by author, 2015), CreateSpace.

41. 1 Corinthians 1:21.

42. 1 Corinthians 2:9.

kingdom will certainly never be revealed. But at the point where our thinking gives us no way forward or no hope, when we let go of this kind of thinking—precisely at that time God's kingdom opens, God's measuring stick is revealed. Concerning the words from the Bible that I quoted above, "But it was to us that God made known his secret spirit by means of his Spirit. The Spirit searches everything, even the hidden depths of God's purposes."[43] In other words, whatever we think or say, our nonsensical dualistic thinking doesn't cut it when we stand before God. Our words are meaningless. But when we negate ourselves by opening the hand of thought, we are turned upside down and allowed to enter the world of religion. That means a place where our eyes have never seen, our ears have never heard, and our human mind has never thought of. That is the sole mystery around which the world of true religion revolves. Only when we let go of our deluded self, negating our conditioned self, is when the wisdom of God is spoken for the first time.

However, we usually interpret this word *self-negation* using our conditioned thinking, and so the world of religion is again completely closed to us. This is because we think that we should completely eliminate delusional human desires and discriminative thinking and enter the state of no-thought. Or we may hate our sinful nature and think that we should strictly keep the precepts. In this way, people become neurotic about achieving no-thought or keeping religious precepts. In the end, we come to see that we can't eliminate the mental states and delusions that cloud our minds. At that point, some people just become defiant, saying, "I cannot eliminate delusional desires and illusory thinking. I'm just a deluded human being who values my instincts more than anything

43. 1 Corinthians 2:10.

else, so I'm going to do whatever I want." But protesting this way is totally off the point.[44]

We mustn't forget that self-negation of conditioned human thinking does not mean that we need to forcibly kill our conditioned thinking. Rather, it is that we are simply ruled by the measurement of God. When we do so, God bestows his blessing that is beyond what we are able to comprehend with our ordinary thinking. "Everyone has sinned and is far away from God's saving presence. But by the gift of God's grace all are put right with him through Christ Jesus who sets them free."[45] In the end, entrusting everything to the measurement of God and being led by God's measurement is what religion is all about.

"Those who are led by God's spirit are God's children."[46] Then what is it like to be led by the measurement of God? I will explain later what this means. However, at the same time, the Buddhist religion is different from other religions. Next, I will talk about why we Buddhists don't use the word *God*.

44. Here Uchiyama is saying that there are three possibilities for Zen practioners: (1) we try to stop thinking and achieve complete no-thought; (2) we try to adhere strictly to the Buddhist precepts; (3) seeing that the first two are impossible, we just give up and live according to our desires and illusions. Indeed, even when sitting zazen, it is impossible to stop our minds from thinking. Also, it is impossible to keep all the precepts. For example, according to the precepts we should not kill any living being. But even if we don't kill animals, we need to kill vegetables, which are also living, in order to eat. If we stop eating, then we kill ourselves, also violating the precepts. But we should not give in to despair and take the third option because we will be wasting our life. Sitting zazen in shikantaza or wholeheartedly calling out the names of Kanzeon Bodhisattva or Amida Buddha is not letting our thoughts or actions control our lives. It is returning to our original, nondual self.

45. Romans 3:23–24.

46. Romans 8:14.

8. Before Yardsticks, Part 1
Kannon and "All Beings Will Be Freed"

It was a house deep in the mountains. Snow was piled high on the ground, and we were talking about taking the next day off. It was getting late as we sat near the warmth of the sunken hearth, and I enjoyed listening to the old gentleman tell stories. This man had lived by himself in this remote mountain location for years, earning a meager living by making charcoal. He told many interesting and mysterious tales, so I visited him frequently. I often recall the stories he told that night. The old gentleman talked as he took mouthfuls of roasted sweet potatoes from the hot ashes of the hearth fire.

The God Who Fell from His Throne

In the beginning, there was a god. Of course, since he was a god, he was an absolute being, beyond dualistic thinking. One day he made people in his own image. However, since people weren't real gods, by nature they discriminated between things, constantly talking about this and that, measuring and comparing themselves to others, being jealous, loving, hating and making war with each other—in other words, engaged in dualistic thinking.

The god's heart was pained by the condition of the people he had created, but a child does not understand the loving heart of their parents, and after a while not only did these humans talk among each other, but in the end, they even started saying things directly to this god. In other words, they alternately believed in and doubted the god. When the god saw how these humans were behaving toward him, he decided that only the people who worshiped him were good and became angry at the rest, making up his mind to punish those who did not have faith in him. At that moment, this god himself fell from his throne and disappeared from this world. In other words, when the absolute god began discriminating between the good and bad among the humans he had created, he himself ceased to be absolute.

The old man ended his story by saying that in the museums around the world, one can find all kinds of mummies of such gods that existed in ancient times, that is, the so-called relative absolute being, or the relative being bearing the name of the absolute. "You say that you are from Tokyo, so I'm sure that you have seen quite a few of these kinds of exhibitions of the mummies of these gods."

Listening to the old gentleman's story, I felt that his view of God was certainly unusual. I agreed with some of his ideas. Wondering more about what he meant, I asked him, "Why did the god fall from his throne?" He answered, "This absolute god—that is, a being beyond dualistic discriminating thinking—created humans who are relative beings. The humans discriminate between the absolute and their relative selves, thinking that an absolute god is good and superior whereas relative is bad and inferior. This god was asked all kinds of questions by these humans and, in response, decided who was good or bad. By being the absolute god who thus engaged in discrimination, at the moment he did so he was transformed into a god who discriminated just like his followers. A god who elevates good and loyal believers over bad ones should instead know that rain falls on the righteous and unrighteous alike and not discriminate between them." The old gentleman just laughed and did not say anything in response to my redundant questions. Instead, he told me the following story.

The Monk Who Fell into the Realm of the Asuras While Observing the Precepts

Once upon a time there was a monk who scrupulously observed the precepts. This monk in his innermost heart carried this burdensome feeling that no one observed the precepts as meticulously as he did, and because of that, when he saw his fellow practitioners neglecting them, he felt that there was nothing he could do. He did not say, "That monk violated such and such a precept" or "That monk again turned away from the Buddha's teachings." He didn't say these things out loud, but he thought them to himself. When he died, he was reborn as an *asura*.[47]

I really don't understand why the old gentleman told me this story, but his words brought something to mind. I recalled the historical fact that in 1233 the Catholic Church began a religious inquisition to examine the beliefs of Christians, and when they didn't meet the set standards of belief, they were branded as heretics and were condemned to be burned at the stake. This hunting of heretics continued unabated, and at one time several hundred people at once were burned at the stake or were forced to convert by being cruelly tortured.

In 1600, Giordano Bruno, the Italian philosopher, astronomer, and mathematician, was condemned to be burned at the stake. If his trial was linked to the earlier inquisition, then this age of religious terror appears to have continued for quite some time.

There was no doubt that these heretics would descend directly to hell when they died. However, because they were burned at the stake, Christians believed that their eternal souls would be purified and thereby saved. The Roman Catholic Church appears to have said that it believed

47. Demigods or titans, mythical beings who are jealous of devas, or higher-level gods. Asuras above all are addicted to evil passions, especially wrath, pride, envy, insincerity, falsehood, boasting, and bellicosity.

burning them at the stake was an act of love. I have to say that these incidents were nothing but fanatical acts.

In essence, the Roman Catholic Church of that time, in the name of absolute love, and being in opposition to the so-called heretics, were themselves just engaged in malice against the opposition in a relative conflict. They were like the god who fell from his throne, or the precept-observing monk who fell into the realm of the asuras. As I was remembering this history, the old man told me another tale.

The Monks Who Became Sleeping Dragons on Mount Muga

Once upon a time, there was a big mountain called Mount Muga.[48] Legend held that on this mountain there was a miraculous tree called Daigo that was not found on other mountains. If you ate the fruit of this tree, your mind would suddenly become clear and open, you would dance with joy, you would gain total confidence, and you would lose all fear.

All sorts of monks, both high and low rank, searched for the Daigo tree on the mountain. However, because they didn't know which tree was Daigo, the monks started to act exactly like wild dogs scrounging food from a garbage can. They began to eat the fruit from any tree, hoping this tree or that tree was the Daigo tree. They got big bellyaches and vomited up what they had eaten. Nevertheless, since they believed in the legend that if they ate of the fruit of the Diago tree they would achieve peace, bliss, and freedom from doubt, even if they had to suffer, they determinedly searched the forest with all their strength trying to find the tree.

At long last, one of the monks discovered the Daigo tree and, having eaten its fruit, became a so-called reclining dragon, attaining sudden enlightenment.

48. Mount Muga is written 無我山, literally "No-Self Mountain." This story is an allegory illustrating the folly of seeking to attain sudden enlightenment. Enlightenment is not about gaining some state of bliss but rather about stripping away our egotistical self and discovering the true self by constant practice.

Wait, what are you talking about? He didn't become any reclining dragon there on Mount Muga after eating the Daigo fruit! He was just a man who followed his own self-centered way.[49]

Someone took pity on these foolish monks and put up a huge signboard saying, "You mustn't bring your small ego-self with you when you enter Mount Muga!" But, as you might expect, there are still people who are taken in by this tale, and they hope for personal gain—that their mind will suddenly become clear and open, they will dance with joy, and they will lose all confusion.

The old gentleman told a very interesting fairy tale. So, shall we leave it here? At this point we have used the words *absolute*, *god*, *precepts*, *love*, *enlightenment*, and *no-self*. Religion undoubtedly is about the problems presented by these words, and they are indeed difficult problems. Since human intellect is subjective, we can easily understand when we hear stories about winning and losing and gain and loss, but when we hear stories about the absolute, such as no win or no loss, or no gain and no loss, the words fail to communicate, like a phone call that can't get through. Trying to explain this concept of the absolute using the human intellect provokes a logical contradiction.

Everyone longs for the absolute, but all we have are tales and legends, or else dogma and ecclesiastical authority that order us how to think. These actually separate us further from the truth of the absolute, and the god that is foisted on us is nothing more than a mummy in a museum. It would be fine if it were just an image of a god lying quietly in a glass case. But when a religious group creates a statue of the god and places it on a palanquin, carrying on and celebrating a festival like we do in Japan, well, that kind of religious nuttiness has existed in all eras. They carry that palanquin with the image on their shoulders, and charlatans

49. This is a pun. "Sleeping dragon" 臥竜 and "self-centered way" 我流 are both pronounced *garyu* but written with different characters.

who are just trying to make a quick buck end up infusing society with the poison of false religion.

It seems that people in India long ago recognized the logical contradiction of the theory of the absolute. Limited by human language, they could only hint at the absolute by describing it in negative terms, using words like *emptiness* or *without fixed nature*. But these words point to nothing other than existence as opposed to nothingness, and relative versus absolute. At that point, changing this into words, we have expressions such as "true reality of all things" or "all phenomenal things are themselves the ultimate reality"—in other words, things just as they are. Wow, this is really complicated!

At this juncture, even these words do not hit the mark; we can take even these negative expressions as being the intellectual constructions of humans. I think that this is living one's life in the comfort of narrow-minded seclusion or living your life in an absolute way with the selfishness of annihilating body and extinguishing mind (wisdom). This is not living with things as they are. If we say that human nature just as it is is good, that means we are completely ignoring the shameful aspects of human nature, such as depravity, corruption, and so forth. This is the current condition of the modern Buddhist world.

In other words, we should not be deceived by names or words or doctrines or myths. Rather, we must open our eyes to the question of what exactly reality is. As long as we don't come up against reality, that is nothing more than holding on to words like the ghost of the absolute. If we can meet up with reality, then it is okay to use words. But what is reality?

It is said in "Xinxinming," or "Faith in Mind,"[50] that the ultimate way is not difficult, it only hates picking and choosing. We read that "the true [or ultimate] path is not difficult." This means that the way is not to be

50. Ch. "Xinxinming," or in English, "Faith in Mind," or sometimes translated "On Clarifying Mind," a poem attributed to Sengcan, the Third Ancestor of Chan Buddhism.

found on the path of profound doctrine or dogma or in the appearance of the absolute that we have been talking about, but it is actually a wide road that opens right in front of us. And this wide road "hates picking and choosing"—that means not measuring everything with our human yardstick, not discriminating with our human intellect.

Instead of getting caught up in words and expressions like *God* or *emptiness* or *things as they are*, "Xinxinming" clearly teaches us that the attitude we need to take is to live out the reality of life right here and right now. As long as we all hold on to our own yardsticks, we are caught up in duality of discriminative thinking.

At another point in "Xinxinming," there is the phrase "abstain from views." When we read this profound teaching, we ask how can we actually "stop choosing," and how do we "abstain from views"? The act of thinking about this is in itself actually nothing other than picking and choosing and having points of view. First, we should not engage in abstaining from views by resolving not to think "What should I do?" and "Can I really do that?" Instead, not choosing, and abstaining from views, is not forcing yourself to stop, but rather it comes before choices materialize or before we measure with our personal yardsticks.

> It is like a babe in the world,
> in five aspects, complete;
> It does not go or come,
> nor rise nor stand.
> "Baba wawa"—
> is there anything said or not?[51]

51. "Song of the Jewel Mirror Samadhi." San Francisco Zen Center. https://www.sfzc.org/files/daily_sutras_Song_of_the_Jewel_Mirror_Samadhi.

9. Before Yardsticks, Part 2
Perceiving and Freeing All Beings from Their Suffering

In Case 52 in the *Book of Serenity*, the following questions and answers are recorded:

> Caoshan asked elder De, "'The [B]uddha's true reality body is like space: it manifests form in response to beings, like the moon in the water'—how do you explain the principle of response?"
>
> De said, "Like a donkey looking in a well."
>
> Caoshan said, "You said a lot indeed, but you only said eighty percent."
>
> De said, "What about you, teacher?"
>
> Caoshan said, "Like the well looking at the donkey."[52]

Here, the reason why Master Caoshan said "The Buddha's true reality body is like space" is because, when speaking about the Buddha, somehow there is something wanting. When we think that we are grateful for the precious virtue of the Buddha, this thought is produced by the yardstick of our conditioned human thinking. That's not right! The virtue of the Buddha and his enlightenment has nothing to do with human beings' petty desires, cravings, or dissatisfactions. This is exactly

52. Thomas Cleary, trans., *Book of Serenity: One Hundred Zen Dialogues* (Boston: Shambhala Publications, 1998), 219. Slightly revised.

like trying to search for limitless, incalculable empty space in the wrong neighborhood.

The Buddha's true Dharma body is like empty space; there is no discrimination, like the well looking at the donkey. It is beyond human desires and our thinking minds. When we hear such teachings, we may think that the buddhas are not focused on anything, are without function, and do not work or make efforts for themselves or others. But Kanzeon Bosatsu functions without seeing objects and without discrimination. As is written in the Diamond Sutra, "You should arouse the mind without attaching to anything,"[53] while not adhering to a point of view or to a particular disposition—for example, it is something like the moon in water. By the way, asking how to respond to and speak about the depth of Buddha, we could say that it is like a donkey looking down a well, but also it is like the well looking up at the donkey.

In other words, as I said before, Kanzeon perceives things from the point of view of looking at the world before applying subjective human yardsticks, so here I use the expression "the well looking up at the donkey" in the same way. In our own minds, even if we think, "What the heck am I going to do? There is no one on this earth more pitiable or unhappy than me," and are exasperated by these kinds of feelings, like the donkey, we are peeking down into the well that is inherently without a yardstick. Or the well without a yardstick is just reflecting the image of the donkey. That is, the well that doesn't measure with the yardstick of conditioned human thinking is just perceiving; this is what I mean by perceiving the world like Kanzeon.

Recently a young woman from a well-to-do family visited me and told me that she was troubled. Even though she wasn't experiencing any particular difficulties in her everyday life, she had built up some serious anxiety and said, "I want to commit suicide." To this I replied, "Okay,

53. Unpublished translation by Shohaku Okumura from the Kumarajiva translation from Sanskrit into Chinese.

that's fine. There are more than enough people in Japan nowadays, so if you die that will save the cost for your food and increase food portions for everyone. Can I ask you to please assign me your portion of food in your will before you commit suicide?" She stared at me with mouth agape. A little later she sent me a letter: "When you said that to me, I felt like a bird that couldn't fly after having its feathers plucked."

Well, it is human nature that if we get some sympathy when we tell our troubles to someone, we persist. But if we continue to complain, then in the end we run into a dead end and there is no resolution. This is the essence of the suffering inherent in human nature and is the merit of the limitless true reality body (*dharmakaya*) of the Buddha.

One time I was returning home from my *takuhatsu*, or alms rounds, which hadn't gone well that day. Just at that moment a student who had been waiting for me approached me. I yelled out, "If these Kyoto people don't want to give me anything on my begging rounds, then I'll just go on strike and won't do them the favor of begging here!" The student responded, "Hey, don't do that. No one will even care if you go on strike." That's right—in order for a strike to have an effect and be worth your trouble, it has to inconvenience someone. If you plan to go on a hunger strike, you need to find the person that you want to cause trouble for, put on a white headband and sit down in front of them, get your picture in the newspaper and get on TV—that is, take actions that are worth doing. If I were to strike because of my unsuccessful begging, then the only person to starve would be me, and the people of Kyoto wouldn't think anything of it. A strike in which you prowl about incognito and starve doesn't sound very appealing. My takuhatsu life is a life in which I am unable to strike. After that, I decided not to yell out in a lone loud voice, "Hey, I'm on strike." Instead of that, whether someone offered me something or not, I continued walking the roads on my alms rounds.

This also pertains to Buddhist practice. If you want to practice zazen and become enlightened, or perhaps become a famous person like the swordsmen Musashi Miyamoto and Tesshu Yamaoka,[54] then you will become eager to go to a Zen temple. There you'll practice zazen while the teachers encourage you: "Yes, yes. That spirit is very important. Do zazen in that spirit; you must do zazen nonstop to achieve enlightenment." Furthermore, they say things like, "You came to the right place. Yeah, just a little bit more. You're within a hairsbreadth of getting enlightened." This kind of talk motivates you to continue your efforts. But, as Sawaki Roshi said, there's no point, no goal or target, in doing zazen. All you need to do is just sit zazen—just sitting for many years or many decades, just try it, setting yourself free from attaining any goals.

Most people quit when they don't have a goal. But, when there is no goal, and you sit and really immerse yourself in zazen without release, then zazen becomes zazen, and practice becomes practice, and the self becomes the self. As it says in the Heart Sutra, "Avalokiteshvara Bodhisattva when practicing deeply the Prajna Paramita"—this is form put into practice. That is the bodhisattva that perceives the self as the self, just practicing in emptiness completely without any goal. If you do zazen with motivation and desire, you are practicing within the realm of your human nature. If you have an enlightenment experience in that realm, even if you think you have attained some special spiritual level, it goes without saying that you have not attained the realization of the Buddha. Master Linji Yixuan repeatedly said, "You students of the Way need to seek a true understanding of the Way." Hearing these words, confused people say, "Yeah! You must attain realization at any cost!" With this as a goal, with the thought of gaining satisfaction, like a horse pulling a cart, they break into a run. But that is completely in the territory of human nature. At the same time, Linji also said, "Stop running around chasing after things!" So now we're completely confused about Linji's meaning! Weren't we told to seek realization and then told to stop chasing it? We

54. Musashi Miyamoto (1584–1645) and Tesshu Yamaoka (1836–1888) were famous samurai swordsmen who also practiced zazen.

come to think that Zen training consists of this suffering of constantly going around and around in circles, and there are some people who say that they have lost their minds many times and even boast about experiencing unusual psychological states. Well, it takes all kinds. However, we need to think of a way to practice in a more relaxed manner.

This "true understanding" that Linji talked about is not something that we measure with our human yardsticks but is instead the truth measured by the yardstick of the Buddha. Since Buddha nature can only be known by buddhas, realization based on our lame ideas cannot possibly be realization. Linji's words are not mistaken: "Stop running around chasing after things!" Remember what we discussed before about the existence of God, the absolute being. The same would apply here. Realization, a true understanding, is the realization of the Buddha. The realization of the Buddha is the same as the knowledge of the absolute god. Accordingly, as long as it's "absolute knowledge," as an object of worship that we must seek, at a minimum it mustn't be a word that we humans say freely. If we must freely express in words this seeking of an object of worship explicitly, then we can say, "that over there" according to our illusions. Surely, if we attain realization, then we can think that we are probably important and distinguished and stop chasing an object of worship, and just make up supposed realization at the level of relative knowledge and change things around.

Realization based on absolute knowledge probably can only be said to be negative (contradictory). We need to carefully reflect on Dogen's logic in the following passage from *Shobogenzo Yuibutsuyobutsu* ("Only a Buddha Together with a Buddha"):

> If realization appears through the force of our thought prior to realization, it must be an unreliable realization. Because realization does not depend on previous thoughts, and it has come from transcending the thought prior to realization, realization is assisted solely by the force of realization. We should know that delusion does not really exist; realization does not really exist.

The "thought before realization" is what I have called the human yardstick. Dogen points out in an exceptionally kind way that as we stand before our human nature, "we should know that delusion does not really exist, realization does not really exist." We accept with gratitude Dogen's guidance. Practicing zazen intently with no target or goal and without desire is shikantaza, or just sitting, and also practice based on verification.[55]

Therefore, the *kan* in Kanzeon means perception before yardsticks, or practicing zazen without a target or goal. Tiantai Zhiyi[56] in his work, *The Essential Meaning of Kannon*, wrote regarding *kan*, "Destroy the forms to which we attach ourselves."[57] This clinging to forms is human nature, that is, the human yardstick. Zhiyi is saying that we need to completely dismantle our picking and choosing, hate and love, and just perceive without our yardsticks. Furthermore, *kan* is also in the Heart Sutra as, "[Avalokiteshvara] clearly saw that all five aggregates are empty."[58] The Diamond Sutra says, "You should view all created things like this."[59] In the Lotus Sutra we read, "All phenomenal things are themselves the ultimate reality" and "the Buddha's realization."

55. This is an expression used by Dogen in *Bendowa* ("On the Endeavor of the Way"). The common translation of this phrase is "practice based on enlightenment," but Okumura Roshi feels that the word *verification* is more accurate and appropriate.

56. See chapter 2.

57. Or "Destroying our attachments to the forms." Both are unpublished translations by Okumura Roshi.

58. The five aggregates or *skandhas* are form, sensation, perception, formation, and consciousness.

59. These lines come at the end of Red Pine's translation of the *Diamond Sutra* (Berkeley, CA: Counterpoint Press, 2001), 27: "As a lamp, a cataract, a star in space, an illusion, a dewdrop, a bubble, a dream, a cloud, a flash of lightning, view all created things like this." In Mu Soeng's translation (Somerville, MA: Wisdom Publications, 2000), 155: "So you should see all of the fleeting world: / A star at dawn, a bubble in the stream, / A flash of lightning in a summer cloud, / A flickering lamp, a phantom, and a dream."

Bankei Zenji[60] expressed *kan* as "the unborn mind of the Buddha." Well, there are many expressions of this in Buddhism. For sure, this *kan* (observation, perception) corresponds to the expression in the Lotus Sutra, "they all will be freed," and in the Heart Sutra, "freed from all suffering."[61] As I have already said, the emancipation of the bodhisattva from the anguish and suffering caused by our human nature can't be solved by money. From the start, it is the resolution of a fundamental problem—dismantling the human yardstick, or even human nature itself. At that point it is also "letting go of body and mind."[62]

Therefore, being freed from suffering is not a matter of having some kind of clear realization or *satori*. Fundamentally it is not based on this stuff of the human yardstick or our subjective thoughts. This good and bad of the human yardstick is only a question of luck, but being freed from suffering goes beyond luck. So, if there is virtue to be found, it is the virtue that can be seen from the point of view of the realization of the Buddha, that is, the yardstick of the absolute. "The virtue of the Buddha is boundless like empty space."[63] No matter how much we grope around for it, we will be dissatisfied and never run up against being freed from suffering. So, if we think that religion will cure our illness, or we have confidence in a realization and can remain unperturbed by life, these kinds of measurements of what is "good" are simply based on our human yardstick. They are not as good as the realization of the Buddha.

60. Bankei Yotaku (1622–93) was a Japanese Rinzai master best known for his talks on what he called the Unborn, one of the most original developments in Zen. According to D. T. Suzuki, Bankei, Dogen, and Hakuin are the most important Zen masters in Japanese history.

61. "The Bodhisattva Avalokiteshvara, while deeply practicing prajnaparamita, clearly saw that all the five skandhas are empty and is thus freed from all suffering."

62. This is Dogen's expression, literally "to drop off body and mind." Uchiyama Roshi would say "to let go of the hand of thought and just sit zazen without any goal or aim."

63. I was unable to find the text that this well-known phrase comes from. The phrase is common in Japan and China.

The Kannon-gyo says that by simply chanting *Namu Kanzeon Bosatsu* we will be freed from all suffering. But in fact, if we chant when we are poor or sick and are hoping for relief, this is not really calling out the name of Kannon. In those situations, we are calling out from the point of view of our human nature, because we are unable to enter fully into the immeasurable and boundless realm on our own. Before we apply our human yardstick, even if we don't think that chanting has any effect, just saying "I take refuge in the sound of the bodhisattva who perceives the world" is what is meant by Buddhist faith and practice. Or, in the words of my poem in my postscript to the Kannon-gyo, "Even though I don't perceive it . . . because Kanzeon can instantly deliver me from suffering, therefore I wholeheartedly chant the name."[64]

I mean, it is part of human nature to suppose that we can use money to completely escape suffering, but that is not truly being freed from suffering. Instead, the true state of freedom from suffering must exist beyond our human perception, beyond simply "I get it." In other words, it is beyond our standard conditioned thinking. Yes, but maybe we don't need what is beyond our perception or even the merit of the Buddha's wisdom. But that is the yardstick of the "me" of our conditioned thinking that says that. Indeed, as long as we think with our own ideas, no matter what we say, we are always applying the yardstick of our prejudiced thoughts. As long as we use our human thinking we will just go around in circles. Only through practicing in a place that is beyond the measurement of our human conditioned thoughts, becoming one with the name of Kanzeon or Amida, or practicing shikantaza will we actualize practice beyond our small minds.

64. See appendix 2.

The Japanese poet-monk Ryokan,[65] suffering from dysentery and too weak to practice zazen, instead took to chanting the nenbutsu ("I take refuge in the vow of Amida Buddha"). He wrote the following poem near the end of his life:

> Since mind and words cannot reach the Pure Land because it is
> so far away,
> without thinking I chanted the name of Amida Butsu.

This is the kind of poem that fully reveals the spirit of the Kannon-gyo. These days, Ryokan's poetry and calligraphy are widely talked about as art, but the real Ryokan was a Dharma descendant of Dogen and practiced seriously. Even this single poem shows how he lived a truly religious life.

65. Taigu Ryokan (1758–1831). A beloved Japanese Soto monk, poet, and renowned calligrapher. He rejected living in a temple and lived by himself in a small hut on a mountainside where he did zazen, went on alms rounds, wrote poetry, and played with the children from the nearby village.

10. The Sound of Silence[66]

We are admonished time and again about noise pollution, and it goes without saying that noise pollution is a product of the violence of the twentieth century. However, even worse than the noise pollution in the outside world is the noise pollution in our own heads. We are constantly seized by all kinds of thoughts that float up, but our thoughts are invariably dressed up in words. My thoughts are clothed in Japanese, while the thoughts of Americans and Britons are clothed in English. I have heard that Japanese who have lived for a long time in America or the UK or in another English-speaking country sometimes talk in their sleep in both Japanese and English—so these people even dream in both languages.

Even though there are various languages, in the depth of these languages there is an underlying meaning. To be accurate, our thoughts are meaningful ideas, so perhaps it is correct to think that these meanings are clearly collected in these languages. However, while meanings are captured by language, since these words, when spoken, are without a doubt sound, when our thoughts suddenly float up into our minds, naturally the sound of the words must construct an image in our minds.

This sound further becomes a voice and then presents as a word. But even when no one is speaking, our minds construct various sounds that come and go in our heads. We have thoughts like the following: "What should I do? Maybe I should do this or that?" or "Maybe it's like this or that?" or "At this point I guess that I'll be able to manage somehow" or "It seems there's a solution" or "I don't like that guy" or "I feel that she likes me" or "The next time I have some money, I want to buy that" or

66. This chapter title comes from a Japanese phrase meaning "nirvana is tranquility."

"That jerk stuck me with that job" or "I'm tired of living" or "I have a hazy feeling and can't settle down." As I said before, even if these thoughts and feelings don't take the clear shape of a word or sound, they do form into meanings and construct sounds that thoroughly take on agreed-upon forms.

Furthermore, I think that the form of this sound mainly has to do with grasping and rejecting, picking and choosing, hating and loving, and making discriminations and choices. That is, the sound of grasping at the world, the sound of rejecting the world, the sound of hating the world, the sound of loving the world, the sound of detesting the world, the sound of attachment to the world—these are, after all, the discriminating, dualistic sounds of the human experience. If we were to analyze these words, we would find they are the voice of our human nature calling out, grasping and rejecting, picking and choosing, based on measurements taken with our human yardstick.

In contrast, when we chant the name of Kanzeon Bosatsu, we take refuge in the sound of the One Who Perceives the Sounds of the World. True perceiving, or hearing, as I explained previously, is something that happens before we grasp or reject, before we employ our yardsticks. Therefore, the sound that perceives the world is separate from discriminations and dualistic thinking and is the sound before we begin discriminating. It is taking refuge in the sound beyond our discriminating mind. Believing in and going forward by entrusting in the unity of mind and body—that is what is meant when we chant the name Kanzeon. In other words, instead of saying this or that and listening to the noise in our heads, we make a quiet sound, *Namu Kanzeon* ("I take refuge in Kanzeon"), and when we take refuge in this sound with our entire body and mind, wholeheartedly just take refuge in and become one with this sound, then calling the name Kanzeon (the Sound That Perceives the World) is actualized. Therefore, needless to say, chanting the name Kanzeon is actually not limited to calling out this particular sound. Also, the sound of chanting *Namu Kie Sanbo* ("I take refuge in the Three Treasures"—that is, in the

Buddha, Dharma and Sangha), or the sound of chanting *Namu Amida Butsu* ("I take refuge in Amida Buddha"), as long as the attitude of this chanting does not come from our selfish desires, all of these are the same as calling out the name of Kanzeon. The Lotus Sutra defines Kanzeon as follows: "By wholeheartedly calling his name . . . all would be freed, that is why the bodhisattva is named Perceiver of the Cries of the World."[67] In other words, that is why we call out the name of Kanzeon with an attitude separate from our petty selves.

If we think about this in a broader sense, we could say that even poetry and music are, to a certain extent, Kanzeon. There is a common Japanese poetic expression: "Keep sunshine in your heart and a song on your lips." Indeed, we humans are often comforted by poems and music, and that is because they also are the sound that perceives the world—that is, Kanzeon.

But if we're still measuring everything by our selfish human yardstick, then we say such things as, "No one is as unhappy as I. I was born like this; I never have any fun." When we start to make this world-loathing noise, we inevitably drive ourselves into a corner. Can we call this self-induced sadism? With our thoughts we make ourselves unhappy because we are attached to the idea of trying to satisfy ourselves.

We start making sounds like, "That guy doesn't take me seriously. I'm insulted," followed by "The next time I see him, I'll tell him off. I'll take my revenge." At the bottom of all this is the desire to be satisfied, which fuels these feelings of anger and drives one to a terrible hysterical outburst. Or else we say, "I've fallen in love with her" and "I want to make her mine." All this noise begins with our picking and choosing, loving and hating, and our desire to be satisfied. We are driven by these feelings to the point that they are beyond our control. If at that time you relax your mind by listening to quiet music, for example, or singing a hymn or a Buddhist pilgrim's song, even chanting a traditional recitation from

67. Reeves, *Lotus Sutra*, 371.

Japanese *bunraku*,[68] you cut off the noise coming from your discriminating mind. This music or song is wholly the sound that perceives the world. For sure, it is like chanting "I take refuge in Kanzeon."

On the contrary, if we sing only when we are happy, then once dissonance breaks out in our mind we say, "This is no time to sing songs," and we certainly forget about singing. Of course, that is not Kanzeon; it is just a pleasant hobby. The religion of Kanzeon is not a hobby or an idle amusement but is devoted to the problem of the self. But the self does not live amid this cacophony of love and hate and discrimination. The self is discovered within the sound that perceives the world. According to your attitude, hymns, choral music, piano, or symphonies can all be the sound that perceives the world; they can all become religion. But at the same time, depending on your attitude, God, Buddha, religious faith, and zazen can be only a hobby and a pastime. Among those who visit temples there are some who say things like, "I just love religion" or "Zen temples are really cool." I have never met a truly religious person who says something like that. But I suppose it is natural for people who take religion as a hobby or a Zen temple as a sightseeing destination.

We understand that, from the standpoint of religion, it is more suitable to be plain or subdued rather than flashy or garish. The more our hobbies and amusements become showy, the more easily the plain and simple ones get mixed up and confused. For example, chanting Buddhist sutras seems to be more effective for delivering us from the cacophony of our conditioned human thinking and our propensity toward hate and discrimination than listening to music by a heavy metal rock band.

Suppose you are walking down the road feeling totally exhausted both physically and emotionally, and then you unexpectedly hear the music of a heartfelt and pure hymn coming from a church, or a lonely echo of a voice coming from a temple quietly chanting a sutra—somehow you feel nostalgic for the spirit of your hometown. Haven't you experienced this?

68. Japanese puppet theater.

A well-known Japanese poem[69] says,

Although it is not yet snowing,
I am saddened by the snow-laden sky in this desolate wintry
scene,
from inside a window,
I hear a solitary voice chanting a sutra.

I feel as if the world of sound is indeed shrouded in unfathomable mystery.

In the same way that such thoughts are liberated by sounds, it is also possible to sit in a posture that manages our body and mind.[70] That is, managing the posture of our bodies, we can divert our ever-present and unavoidable evil passions, carnal desires, and wild ideas.

By way of comparison, think about a dog that is always chained up and barks hysterically and becomes high-strung. This happens because the dog has no outlet for its excess energy. A dog that is not always chained and is freer to move its body doesn't bark hysterically because it can appropriately dissipate this energy. In the case of a guard dog, I don't

69. I could not locate the source of this poem, but it is safe to say that Uchiyama Roshi did not compose it himself.

70. Uchiyama Roshi talks about the zazen posture and how it is an important feature not only of sitting practice but also in traditional Japanese arts like tea ceremony and flower arranging. In *Opening the Hand of Thought,* Uchiyama compares the upright posture of zazen to the posture of Rodin's *The Thinker*. Uchiyama describes the hunched pose of *The Thinker* as "caught up in delusion," whereas someone sitting zazen is in a posture conducive to letting go of thought. He describes the upright posture of zazen as a unique legacy of the East, as opposed to the Western tradition of *The Thinker*, which comes to us from the Greek philosophical tradition. *The Thinker* is bent over with gnarled, taut muscles and caught up in his deluded musings, while the sitter is sitting comfortably in an upright posture, supporting the spine on the secure base of the folded legs. By managing our posture, we can focus more clearly on what we are doing and free ourselves from our disorderly conditioned thinking.

know which is better, but it goes without saying that for the dog itself, it is better to be a free dog that is raised outdoors in more natural conditions than a pet dog that is kept indoors on a tatami mat.

Similarly, that is why it is good for young people to participate in outdoor sports. A young person who sits at home eating greasy food, absorbed in reading pornographic and prurient romantic novels or morbid detective stories, of course doesn't have a decent outcome. Sports play a vital role in converting and diffusing this energy, and at the same time they promote the development of a healthy body and mind. Giving a young person too much leisure time is not good, and in the end it fosters evil passions and carnal desires. Sports can help young people manage their bodies by perceiving the world.

For a refined or older person, quietly arranging flowers or preparing matcha (green tea) can have the same effect as sports has for a young person. Instead of spending time gossiping or badmouthing the neighbors, doing flower arranging or tea ceremony is much better. However, the important thing is our attitude. If we play sports just for the sake of maintaining a healthy body, or if we do tea ceremony just for the sake of tea ceremony, then we are managing our posture by perceiving the world. However, if we play sports to be victorious or to break records, or if we do tea ceremony to gain social status, then we are managing our body with dualistic thinking and for our own selfish desires. In any event, for the sake of religion it is better to engage in plain and quiet actions. Rather than doing sports, tea ceremony, or flower arranging, there is nothing better or more appropriate than sitting zazen in the full lotus posture as a way to perceive the world by managing our bodies.

If we find ourselves increasingly craving satisfaction and engaging in self-centered behavior, in the end, rather than letting these things become unmanageable, we can divert our minds by engaging in physical activity. That is a healthy and realistic way to resolve these feelings. Human civilizations in various regions came to understand this since early times.

Sporting events in ancient Greece were originally consecrated to the gods, and we know that music in many cultures developed for religious purposes. Even tea ceremony began as a ceremony offering tea to the Buddha.[71] Flower arranging began as offering flowers to the Buddha at a temple. In other words, these actions themselves are attempts to divert human delusions by physical actions, dedicated to gods and offered to the Buddha because they were thought to be suitable. Even though these activities were previously worthy of the gods, we currently live in spiritually bankrupt times.

These days, sports, music, tea ceremony, and flower arranging have become as important to people as religion. Even petty games, records of sports exhibitions and spectacles, lascivious coquetry, and vain genteel pastimes have all been given importance equal to religion. In contrast to this, the Asian traditions of India, China, and Japan have methods to transform human delusions through physical action. That method is given the name "practice" and has been polished and refined over a long time.

I want to draw attention to some of these practices that stem from our unique Eastern culture. As I have said, music and sports themselves can interrupt the human delusions of grasping and rejecting. But we as humans have instead used them to take joy in our delusions so that, before we know it, they have progressed into depravity and corruption. In opposition to this common trend, in the East we have cultivated an attitude of distancing ourselves from the delusions of grasping and rejecting and love and hate by not using the measurements that inhabit our minds. Instead, we learn to see things that are happening here and now, cutting off our delusions through the perfection of a pure practice. When we wholeheartedly chant the name of Kanzeon or do zazen, we are surely performing this kind of practice.

In the next chapter I would like to continue my discussion of what is meant by "one mind" or "wholeheartedly" or "becoming one with."

71. Even today, during sesshins, practitioners often have tea together in a formal way.

We lose the true meaning of practice if we think of it as only using our bodies as a handy means to transform our delusions or attain spiritual health. Instead, our practice just becomes the Sound That Perceives the World (Kanzeon) or the Zazen Posture That Perceives the World (the body of Kanzeon). It is just the sound of the universe and the dignified, pious posture that penetrates the entire universe.[72]

Truly, we must also say that Kanzeon is the sound of the self becoming only the self. And, in wholeheartedly chanting the name of Kanzeon and just sitting (shikantaza) we finally find the practice that allows us to return to the true form of the self.

"Even though I don't perceive it, Kanzeon is functioning within me. Therefore, I wholeheartedly chant the name."[73]

In this practice, there is no human sentiment at all. Rather, human sentiment has been transformed into the sound that comes from the universe and into the dignified posture of the entire universe.

It is truly a wonderful thing that in the East we have discovered and refined this sophisticated universal practice, in contrast with many other cultures, which have facilitated the development of worldly human passions and delusions, achieving nothing more than needlessly complicating people's lives.

72. *Jinkenkon no igi* can be translated as "the dignified refined pious posture and presence that penetrates the entire universe." Reference to the phrase *igi* (威儀) is found in Case 381 ("Wisdom Is Not the Way") in *Dōgen's Extensive Record* (Somerville, MA: Wisdom Publications, 2010), 333. The passage refers to when Sariputra was first drawn to Buddhism. While walking in the street, he perceives Aśvajit, a disciple of the Buddha, on his alms rounds. Sariputra is drawn to Aśvajit's "dignified bearing and refined elegance." *Igi* is also the subject of *Shobogenzo Gyobutsu Iigi* ("The Dignified Conduct of Practice Buddha").

73. This is a line from Uchiyama Roshi's postscript poem at the end of this book. Since our mundane human consciousness is incapable of perceiving Kanzeon, we single-mindedly chant the name, and by wholeheartedly carrying out this practice, Kanzeon actualizes within us.

11. "One Mind"

The Priceless Absolute Reality Actualizes in the Present Moment

Bodhisattva Inexhaustible Mind asked this question of the Buddha, "World-Honored One, for what reason does the Bodhisattva Perceiver of the Cries of the World have the name Perceiver of the Cries of the World?" In answer to this question, the Buddha replied, "Good son! If there were countless hundreds of thousands of billions of living beings experiencing suffering and agony who heard of the Bodhisattva Perceiver of the Cries of the World, and wholeheartedly called his name, Bodhisattva Perceiver of the Cries of the World would immediately hear their cries, and all of them would be freed . . . This is why the bodhisattva is named Perceiver of the Cries of the World."[74]

Therefore, with regard to the complete question-and-answer, we have the suffering of living beings, followed by all living beings being freed from their suffering by the Perceiver of the Cries of the World, and one by one appreciating the religious meaning of wholeheartedly calling out or chanting the name.

When we hear the phrase "wholeheartedly call out the name" of Kanzeon Bosatsu, no one would think this word *wholeheartedly* (*isshin* 一心, which also translates to "one mind") is particularly difficult to understand. We commonly talk about "studying wholeheartedly" or "nursing someone who is ill wholeheartedly" or "engaging in our work

74. Paraphrased from Reeves, *Lotus Sutra*, 371. See also Watson, *Lotus Sutra*, 298–99.

wholeheartedly." Also, we use phrases such as "with heart and soul" or "intently" or "single-mindedly," and in most cases we mean something like "without looking aside, looking neither right nor left" or "with all one's might" or "with all-out effort." Or it's like becoming fixated on one thing. In other words, we can describe it as losing our heads when we focus on one thing exclusively. So then, how should we use this expression "one mind" or "wholeheartedly"? Just the fact that we need to examine our thinking when we use this expression "one mind" may prove that we are not acting with one mind or wholeheartedly. Rather, not reflecting on ourselves and focusing solely on one thing or idea, when we view things from the point of view of this so-called one mind, it's like we've become drunk. Isn't it like when people become fanatic believers in some kind of new religion?[75] When someone accepts this concept of one mind without thinking about it, this is the root cause of mistaken fanatical religious beliefs.

Thinking calmly about the meaning of one mind or wholeheartedness as unifying our mind—does this really mean focusing our mental effort on one thing? Our minds and our thinking are always scattered in a million different directions. It appears that this term *seishintoitsu*, which means to concentrate the mind, seems to be the reason why many people who practice Zen use the expression, "Zazen is one-pointed concentration." But is it really a simple matter to quiet our minds? I dare say that when it comes to our many scattered and excited thoughts, to somehow calm ourselves and concentrate on a single thought presents us with a thousand contradictions and just ends up making us more confused.

In the "Xinxinming" ("On Clarifying Mind" or "Faith in Mind")—that is, the mind before separation between self and other) we find the following passage: "If you try to stop the comings and goings of your mind, because this intention to stop the movement is another movement,

75. See note 32.

there is no time for your mind to stop."[76] This is not just some theory but if you actually do zazen or call out the name of Kanzeon or Amida Buddha, anyone would undoubtedly experience being troubled by confusion and doubt if they practiced trying to concentrate on a single thing. It's not as easy as twisting several strands of thread together to make one strand, or like waiting for dust to settle. The fact that the more we try to focus on one thing the less we are able to do so is proof of the nature of our mind—and our inability to remain focused as we are constantly generating the next thought. I think that it is possible for people who are easily influenced by suggestion to feel like they are able to concentrate exclusively on one thing, but when this homing in on one thing unravels, we go back to where we started, with all our thoughts bubbling up. This type of single-minded concentration is outside the ken of true religion.

From the perspective of the Buddhadharma, chanting or calling out wholeheartedly doesn't mean chanting with all one's might or being totally engrossed in one thing. It isn't some kind of self-hypnosis. Without a sense of one mind, we can't call any activity a religion. This sense of one mind is necessary for opening the universal gate that frees all living beings from suffering.

We need to be careful about how we go about chanting the name of Kanzeon. It's not focusing our concentration on one thing or doing something with one mind. "One mind" is not an adverb; it is the subject of the sentence. In other words, one mind is calling out the name of Kanzeon. This might be different from what people imagine. But as the *Shobogenzo*[77] says, "One mind is all dharmas and all dharmas are one

76. In other words, if you try to stop your thoughts from coming and going in your head, this very act is also an action that produces more thoughts, so your mind will continue producing thoughts that will never end.

77. *Shobogenzo Sokushinzebutsu* ("Mind Itself Is Buddha").

mind." Or it is the one mind referred to in the Avatamsaka Sutra: "The threefold world is only mind."[78]

Well, the unthinkable has happened! When you first read it, the text appears so straightforward, and it simply means "Call out with all your might." However, we are now complicating things by bringing up the *Shobogenzo* and the Avatamsaka Sutra, saying that all dharmas are mind, or the threefold world is only mind. We have no choice but to bring up these key concepts if we want to discuss the Buddhadharma. For myself, I would like to keep my writing as simple as possible. I know these Buddhist terms are hard to understand, but I can't avoid using them when it comes to talking about the essence of the Buddhadharma.

So, what exactly does it mean to say the threefold world is only mind? The threefold world is the world of desire, the material world (the world of matter and substance), and the nonsubstantial world (the world of the spirit). Therefore, the term "threefold world" can be understood as representing the world we live in, but a problem arises with "the threefold world is only mind." If we make a hasty interpretation, then Buddhadharma suddenly becomes just some form of naive philosophical idealism. Following this interpretation, someone might say that according to Buddhism an automobile that appears directly in front of us is just a phantom in our mind. We could close our eyes and not perceive a car. After all, the Heart Sutra says that matter is not different from emptiness and emptiness is not different from matter. So essentially matter doesn't exist, right? Well, give it a try. You'll be sent flying by that car. If Buddhism were nothing more than some form of simple, naive idealism, then we would be unable to transmit the teachings in modern times. One could say that the Buddhism of ancient times has disappeared from

78. The threefold world is the triple world of desire, material things, and nonmaterial things—that is, samsara, or the world of delusion that we live in, arises from the consciousness of beings and has no separate objective existence. The entirety of the phenomenal world is nothing other than the projection of the mind. Uchiyama here refers to the expression used in the Avatamsaka Sutra, "the triple world is one mind."

the earth. Regarding this point, to understand Buddhist teachings, we need to change our thinking. A good example of this is when we contemplate the word *mind*. Nowadays when we say *mind* we first think of consciousness from the standpoint of psychology. But *mind* in the expression "the threefold world is only mind" is entirely different from consciousness as understood by contemporary psychology. Buddhism uses its own unique terminology.

In Buddhism, when we use the term *mind*, if what we call mind includes the seeing mind and the thinking mind (the functioning consciousness), then at the same time the object being seen (or perceived), or the thought being thought is also mind. In Buddhism, when the word *mind* is used, it means not only the mind that sees or the mind that thinks but also the object that is seen and the thought that is thought. The triple world can only exist for the first time when its function is enabled. Existence is impossible when we cut off the seeing and thinking mind. In other words, all existence is the result of the activity of our mind. Therefore, if the action of seeing is the result of the mind, the object being seen also exists as the intentional existence of the mind. The Buddhist understanding is something different from philosophical idealism. In Buddhism, seeing is the result of mind, and being seen is also the result of mind. Therefore, absolute reality occurs after throwing off subject and object. That is, seeing and being seen are both mind and also the three worlds. We can say that the point at which we wipe away seeing and being seen, subject and object, is the place where seeing with one mind and the threefold world being seen truly becomes "the threefold world is only mind."

Master Menzan[79] said regarding "the threefold world is only mind" prior to the separation of subject and object that we can't place a value

79. Menzan Zuiho (1683–1769) was a Japanese Soto Zen scholar who helped to revitalize Zen practice and reintroduce Dogen's writings. His influence is still felt today.

on the expression "the threefold world is only mind."[80] This comment is eloquent and easy to understand. When we measure with our yardstick, we always separate subject and object. That is, when we place a value on something, we separate the appraisal value in our mind from whatever absolute value the object has. Even if we want to put a value on it, the manifestation of "the threefold world is only mind" is only one indivisible unit, and there is no way to put a price tag on it. That is what "the threefold world is only mind" means.

Then, there is the following passage from Dogen Zenji:

> We clearly understand that the mind refers to the mountains, rivers, and the great earth; the sun, the moon and the stars. However, in what is said here, when we take a step forward, there is something insufficient; and when we take a step backward, there is something extra. The mind of the mountains, rivers and the great earth is only mountains, rivers and the great earth. Outside of them, there are not any waves, wind or smoke. The mind of the sun, the moon and the stars is only the sun, the moon and the stars. Outside of them, there is not any fog or mist. Outside of them, there is no horse or monkey. The mind of a chair and a whisk is only the chair and whisk. Outside of them, there is no bamboo or wood. Because it is thus, "mind itself is buddha" is "mind itself is buddha" without any defilement. All buddhas are all undefiled buddhas.[81]

In other words, the mountains, rivers, and great earth as threefold world is only mind—that is, the mind of the mountains, rivers, and great earth are only the mountains, rivers, and great earth. Furthermore, we

80. Here Uchiyama Roshi paraphrases Menzan's commentary on the three worlds are one mind.

81. *Shobogenzo Sokushinzebutsu* ("Mind Itself Is Buddha"), an unpublished translation by Shohaku Okumura. I have added the last four sentences not included by Uchiyama as I feel they are important to understanding the meaning of Dogen's words.

cannot assess the value of waves, wind, and smoke. The mind of life and death, coming and going, is only life and death and coming and going, and we cannot attach any worth to delusion and realization. And the mind of the four great elements and five aggregates are only the four great elements and five aggregates—and again, we can't set a value on horses and monkeys.

It is precisely because we needn't be concerned about things prior to our comparisons that the threefold world is only mind. Year in and year out, we carry around the judgments we make in our minds. It is human nature to assess value, looking first in this direction and then that direction, loving and hating, saying this is good and that is bad, but understanding this so-called human nature as a manifestation of "the threefold world is only mind" is itself the zazen of the threefold world is only mind. We need to make sure that we understand this.

Returning to what I discussed earlier, "calling out with one mind" can be seen as sitting with "the threefold world is only mind"—and what is that exactly? Thinking about Dogen's words, "the mind in chanting"—that is, chanting with one mind—is only chanting. Also, there is no experiencing of suffering or agony, and all are not freed from suffering and agony. So truly chanting with one mind means chanting without any intent to gain something. Repeating a mantra for the purpose of relieving our suffering is not the true meaning of chanting a mantra. Chanting without attaching any value, without any intent to gain something, is what is meant by chanting with one mind.

Shinran wrote, "I am entirely ignorant as to whether the nenbutsu is really the cause of birth in the Pure Land, or whether it is the karma that will cause me to fall into hell."[82] Truly when chanting the nenbutsu,

82. Shinran (1173–1263) was the founder of the Jodo Shinshu Pure Land school of Buddhism in Japan. This statement is from *Tannisho,* a record of sayings attributed to Shinran, and was translated by the Ryukoku translation group.

I think that Shinran believed that the mind of nenbutsu is just nenbutsu, and that it is neither the Pure Land nor Hell.

Our discussion of one mind has become overly intellectual, but as it is a fundamental truth, I wanted to explain as clearly as possible how we chant with one mind.

12. The Reality without Language and the Undefiled Self

Chanting Wholeheartedly with One Mind

During and right after the war, when food was scarce, not only was it difficult to get food that would fill you up, but the price of kabocha (Japanese winter squash) suddenly jumped up. Probably the reason the price increased was that kabocha grows off season and is sweet, flavorful, nutritious, and filling.

For four or five years after the war, some people made a good profit selling kabocha. One year in particular, many farmers grew a lot of kabocha, thinking they too could make a lot of money. They converted over half of their fields to kabocha, sunk a lot of money into fertilizer, and put all their efforts into it. As a result, they had a huge bumper crop of wonderful kabocha.

Looking at their crop, thinking that they were the gods of good fortune and counting their chickens before they hatched, they each asked themselves, "How much money will I make?" But, as it happened, more food appeared in the markets, and the farmers did not get the prices they had assumed they would. The farmers put the squash in their storehouses, thinking that people would eat kabocha in the winter and so there was no need to sell earlier at a loss. But later when the farmers tried to sell the kabocha, sweet potatoes were available and the price of kabocha had fallen. The farmers were worried. Food prices had changed drastically from the year before, and their profit predictions had completely changed. Standing in front of their storehouses, looking at the mountains of kabocha, the farmers lamented, saying, "It wasn't supposed to happen this way." As for the squashes, they were not affected and were just squashes. The kabocha did not have grief-stricken faces, they weren't apologetic—they were simply kabocha. Such is the nature of squash.

We humans understand that our existence in this world is dependent upon language, but at the same time I find it strange that our way of understanding or point of view is always expressed in words. A person points at another, saying, "that dude," "that gentleman, "that lady," and our choice of words expresses the feelings and emotions that we have for them. To quote a well-known haiku by the poet Basho:

Whenever I speak out
My lips are chilled,
The autumn wind.

Just using words to clearly state our point of view is a losing proposition: we might think that person is annoying us, or they're making a fool of us or speaking in a calculating way, so they can take advantage of us. As you can see, this type of language is negative—not to mention that when we use language to express what we think is good or bad, depending on what we believe, we are naturally unable to hide our point of view when we speak. Or, when we try to speak only objectively about what's good or bad, not including our subjective opinions, it is still just information from our point of view, even if presented like a news report or a scientific finding. But our point of view is nothing more than our opinion and is not our actual circumstances. Because of this, depending on how we deal with our current condition, we can't deny that we are merely expressing our personal viewpoint.

Our viewpoint depends on how we look at something, and our way of looking at it is one-dimensional. We always look at things from our human viewpoint. Don't we always inherently see things through the lens of our organizational systems?

According to Heidegger's philosophy,[83] human existence is being-in-the-world, so humans live according to our explanations and interpretations. We are not just surrounded by things, but by the environment of our world. We do not just look at things but rather consider things as tools to use in our lives. Accordingly, even when we look at a single pine tree, we're not just looking at it, we're seeing it in the context of a pine tree in my garden, for example. Does the shape of the tree enhance my garden? Does it add to the elegance of my surroundings? Does it act as a good windbreak or as an impediment to the expansion of a road? Could I use it for lumber? How many bundles of firewood could I get out of it? We see the tree in terms of the different types of value we place on it. Even when we look at the tree from a scientific or scholarly viewpoint, if we see it as a tool of our scientific pursuits, then we don't value it for anything other than how we as humans see it. As humans, we are apt to confuse our own personal circumstances with the interpretations and values that we place on things.

For example, when evaluating a pig, someone might say, "What a great pig! It's nice and fattened up." This might be the definition of a good pig from the point of view of someone who eats meat. Or someone might say, "The sun rises and sets," but that depends on where your observation point is on the earth. Or you might say, "That guy is obviously rich since he has a luxury car." But the owner might have gone deeply in debt and doesn't have any money now.

However, when we look at things from the perspective of the reality that cannot be expressed with language, a pig is just a pig, neither good nor bad; the sun is just the sun and doesn't actually rise or set. Dogen Zenji wrote about this reality that cannot be expressed in words:

83. *Being and Time*, 1927.

> The mind of the mountains, rivers and the great earth is only mountains, rivers and the great earth. Outside of them, there is no wave, wind or smoke. The mind of the sun, the moon and the stars is only the sun, the moon and the stars. Outside of them, there is no fog or mist.

Paraphrasing Master Menzan, this reality can be described as "the reality that we can't put a price on."

All the uproar about the price of kabocha is based on a value system created by human beings in response to an event. But the face of the kabocha is unperturbed and calm; it expresses the mind of the reality that cannot be expressed in words. I too live within this system of human valuations: love and hate, gain and loss, win and lose, all this commotion. At the point when this "I" that is always perceiving itself no longer perceives this "I," isn't this "I" the reality before language that presents a serene face, just the self being the self?[84] The calm "I" that is one with the triple world as one mind, and also one with the universe and the kabocha.

As Dogen wrote in *Shobogenzo Shoho Jisso* ("The Reality of All Things"),

> This so-called "form of suchness" is not a single form. [That is,] this form of suchness is not just a single [form] of suchness. It is suchness that is immeasurable, boundless, inexpressible, and unfathomable. We should not measure it using a measurement of one hundred or

84. This phrase has many possible translations, including the more literal "the self doing the self." It is an abbreviation of the enigmatic expression originally used by Uchiyama Roshi's teacher Sawaki Roshi: "Zazen is the self selfing the self." See Arthur Braverman's explanation of using the noun *self* as a verb in his excellent book on Sawaki, *Discovering the True Self: Kodo Sawaki's Art of Zen Meditation* (New York: Counterpoint, 2020), 131.

many thousands. We should measure it with the yardstick of all beings; we should measure it with the yardstick of the true reality.[85]

One evening at twilight someone came to me with a hopelessly sad face and said, "I don't have enough money to eat." I said, "I'm sorry to hear that. Here, fill yourself up on this," and I offered him a bowl of brown rice gruel with some vegetables. He made a strange face and said, "I didn't mean that I am hungry." To which I replied, "Well, if you don't eat, you'll be hungry." As our conversation continued, I realized his so-called predicament didn't amount to much when he explained that he lived with his mother and father and that his income was more than twice what our income was at the temple. He was not talking about physical pain from being hungry, but rather he was not able to keep up appearances or engage in vain displays on his salary. Complaining that he couldn't eat was certainly a strange and unnecessary way to describe himself. Thereupon, I proceeded to give him a lecture on his foolishness, saying, "Look at us! There are three of us practicing here in this temple, and we are living on less than half of what you have, and we have no problem eating."

Because of how we are wired as human beings, besides the true character of "the self that is only doing the self," it is also true that there is an "I" that we fabricate from the world around us, and this "I" can become absorbed in the ups and downs of the market and can give itself over to being angry, delighted, or sad. However, that very "I" that is in turmoil, delusion, and darkness based on ignorance can become convinced that this fictional world is the true nature of the self. We need to understand that our true nature is "three worlds are just one mind" and that it is not influenced at all by the rising and falling of world market prices.

However, not only is the true nature of the self "the self that is only doing the self," but I'm delighted that when I face myself in zazen there

85. Unpublished translation by Shohaku Okumura.

can be no market value associated with it. I have often heard people say, "I can't stop being taken prisoner by my mind" or "I can't attain a state of no-thought." Probably these people have heard satori described by someone with a smattering of knowledge about Buddhism in a single phrase, such as "freeing one's imprisoned mind" or "stopping all thought." But when we face our original mind, we say to ourselves, "It doesn't happen that way."

The true nature of the self is "the self that is only doing the self." If we think, "I can't stop being taken prisoner by my mind" or "I'm unable to attain satori," these thoughts are insignificant. Conversely, even when I think, "I've become enlightened" or "I've reached a good place," that indefinable condition is the true form of the self. First, saying "I've reached a good place" or "It's hard to reach enlightenment" is just a wild appraisal made with our personalized human values, and has nothing to do with the true nature of the self. These kinds of thoughts are nothing but wild delusions. Moreover, the true nature of the self that is indifferent to words is the reality of the undefiled self that is not subject to or polluted by wild ideas of value according to the world marketplace—it's just the self doing the self. Because of that, we are unaware of this true form of the self and at the same time definitely nothing new is being created by the efforts of Buddhist practitioners. If we create something new by our practice, then without a doubt that will only collapse. But that's not it. Whether we practice or not—and naturally if our practice does not become polluted—that is the true nature of our original self. However, only through undefiled practice can the undefiled true nature of the self be manifest here right now.

There is always a sound of emptiness ringing out from the true form of the unconditional self, flowing forth, chanting with one mind. Chanting with one mind is chanting from the one mind itself, completely undefiled by the world market price. Furthermore, it is the one mind that is connected to the universe of the three worlds; in other words, that chanting is the "sound that sings out from the cosmos." It doesn't matter whether I try to perceive it or not; this sound reverberates throughout the universe.

"Even though I don't perceive it, Kanzeon is functioning within me. Therefore, I wholeheartedly chant the name."[86] This chanting with one mind is using our mouths to intone and invoke this "sound of undefiled emptiness," unconditioned, just as it is, before we cook it with our thoughts and perceptions.

Shinran established this sound of unconditioned reality, or the true form of the self, as Amida's calling and inviting all sentient beings to take refuge in the original vow of Amida Buddha. That absolute nature can be said to be like the edict of an emperor or heavenly being. Therefore, relying on Amida's vow and chanting the nenbutsu can be called "the nenbutsu of the vow of other-power."[87] However, in this case, even if we call it other-power, of course we don't mean to say the other-power called Amida. If Amida is another being separate from ourselves then we wouldn't be able to put the so-called self-power we employ in chanting the nenbutsu to work. Since we are usually unable to perceive Amida, we refer to this being as other-power, but it is none other than the true form of the self. Because of this, precisely speaking, we need to say that this absolute other-power is also absolute self-power.

In summary, one mind means the "triple world is one mind," something to which no human value can be assigned. Therefore, chanting

86. From Uchiyama Roshi's concluding poem in this book. See appendix 2.

87. *Tariki*, other-power, and *jiriki*, self-power, are traditionally thought to be the forms of practice of Pure Land and Zen, respectively. *Tariki* in Pure Land Buddhism refers to relying on faith in Amida Buddha's vow and chanting *Namu Amida Butsu* to achieve rebirth in the Pure Land. In Soto Zen, practitioners are often described (from the Pure Land perspective) as using self-power to sit shikantaza. However, chanting the nenbutsu also requires self-effort, and shikantaza also requires faith in our sitting practice. Uchiyama Roshi therefore said that they are the same and that chanting the nenbutsu is like "doing zazen with your mouth." In his final years, Uchiyama Roshi had physical difficulties and was unable to sit, so he chanted the nenbutsu and *Namu Kanzeon Bosatsu* instead.

from the standpoint of one mind is chanting with the sound flowing out of the true form of the self, empty and undefiled by any worldly assessment. Another name for chanting with one mind is Kanzeon. True observation is perceiving before applying our yardstick of gain and loss, love and hate. Consequently, "the sound of perceiving the world" is the sound that is empty and uncontaminated by our petty human yardsticks. For that reason, images of Kanzeon often depict the bodhisattva holding a lotus flower. The lotus flower emerging pure from the mud is an established Buddhist symbol. The blooming of the lotus flower represents the purity of our essential buddha-nature.

Even if we don't chant *Namu Kanzeon Bosatsu* to the personification of the bodhisattva, it would seem to be okay to chant, "I take refuge in reality prior to human yardsticks" or "I take refuge in undefiled emptiness." However, chanting either of these expressions attaches a coloring of language, and we then enter the world of human yardsticks and of humans attaching a value or price to something, making them unacceptable as expressions of the world beyond thought. Therefore, there is nothing more we can do except chant *Namu Kanzeon Bosatsu*, actualizing the undefiled sound that perceives the world.

Implicit in chanting the sound, *Namu Kanzeon Bosatsu* is not dependent on language and has no meaning, so by chanting this we can't help but actualize the sound that perceives the world. However, Kanzeon Bosatsu is nothing other than the sound of the true form of the self reverberating out when it connects with the true reality of the universe just as it is; it is certainly one's true self. This true self is undefiled and unsullied, so we have deep reverence for it and chant with one mind.

13. The Buddha Who Practices within Delusion

Shikantaza and Chanting with One Mind

When we sit in the zazen posture, we are truly sitting zazen, and by the same logic when we use our mouths to chant the nenbutsu we are certainly chanting the nenbutsu. But we need to fully understand and be aware that, while the above is true, by simply sitting in the zazen pose we are not necessarily doing zazen, and by chanting the nenbutsu we are not necessarily chanting with one mind. For example, we can think of other things or read the newspaper while we eat, but as long as we are passing the food down our throat, we can say that we are eating. Even so, in the case of the reality of religious practice, we attach more importance to our attitude than to performing the action. We might be sitting in the zazen posture, but we are sometimes not truly engaging in zazen. If we are sleeping while in the zazen posture, anyone would say that we are napping, and it is clear that we are not sitting zazen. It's not a big sin, but sleeping is not true zazen.

The fundamental error, though, is thinking that zazen is a device for attaining satori. But that is not the case. We should remember what Dogen wrote: "If realization appeared through the force of thoughts prior to realization, it would be an unreliable realization."[88] For the most part, sitting practice is presented as something that leads to realization, but that kind of zazen[89] is not real zazen practice, and is just like falling asleep during zazen. Zazen is nothing more than sitting with our legs crossed maintaining our posture with our muscles and bones without delusion or realization. If we are going to use the word *enlightenment*, we should determine that zazen is just zazen, so we can say that sitting zazen is in itself enlightenment, and we must say zazen is the practice of enlightenment.[90] Realization can only materialize in the actual practice of zazen itself. If realization were something that we ourselves were able to perceive and then say, "I'm enlightened," then if that's what we want, that's fine—but it is nothing more than an extension of our deluded human sentiment. The following passage is from Dogen's *Bendowa*:

> If practice and enlightenment were separable as people commonly believe, it would be possible for them to perceive each other. But that which is associated with perceptions cannot be the standard of enlightenment because deluded human sentiment cannot reach the standard of enlightenment.[91]

Many people sit in the zazen posture. For some of them, they have no doubt that zazen is just zazen. This is one reality. But there are people for

88. This passage is from *Shobogenzo Yuibutsuyobutsu* ("Only a Buddha Together with a Buddha") in which Dogen explains that realization or satori "does not depend upon [previous thoughts], and it has come from transcending [the thoughts prior to realization], realization is assisted solely by the force of realization" (unpublished translation by Shohaku Okumura).

89. *Taigozen* is a term used by the Soto School to refer to sitting done for the sake of attaining personal satori or enlightenment.

90. Literally practice based on verification, or the practice of enlightenment. That is, there is no separation between practice (zazen) and enlightenment; zazen is enlightenment, and enlightenment is zazen.

91. Unpublished translation by Shohaku Okumura.

whom practice is not so simple, and they sit for five or ten years and miss the point, complaining, "I haven't attained satori yet." This is another reality. However, it doesn't matter if someone is clever or stupid. It is critical to completely understand that sitting in the zazen posture while you're sleeping or thinking about realization from you own point of view and saying it must be like this or like that—this is not true zazen practice.

In contrast to zazen, which requires the use of your entire body, chanting the nenbutsu wholeheartedly requires only your mouth—the "sound in one's mind." Although Pure Land practitioners describe chanting as an easy practice, in fact it is more difficult than zazen. Shinran especially emphasized faith, and if the believer's attitude becomes disconnected from the nenbutsu practice then the chanting is confused. I have personally witnessed a mother-in-law badmouthing a young wife for never cleaning the toilet, and then proceeding to clean the toilet while chanting maliciously, *Namu Amida Butsu*, *Namu Amida Butsu*. We can call this the nenbutsu of rebuke, or the nenbutsu of a sharp putdown, but we have to say that it bears no relationship with the nenbutsu of gratitude to Amida. We all have these lapses. So, in the case of the nenbutsu, it's not good enough to just recite it with one's mouth. It is crucial that we have faith but because faith is a difficult thing, I think that followers of Shinran have all experienced suffering in connection with their faith and practice, and at least once have let out deep sighs of frustration. In zazen, your entire body actualizes your faith, so there is no easier practice than sitting.

However, zazen practice is also difficult precisely because the practice requires using our whole body and not just our mouth. We must stop sitting zazen when we do physical work. For example, it would not be possible to sit like Bodhidharma facing a wall for nine years without eating or drinking. During that time, it would be good if someone gave you an offering. But these days no one would be eccentric enough to attempt this kind of practice, so in order to carry out a life based on zazen practice you need to do some amount of work. It's also hard for people who work normal jobs to maintain a zazen practice. These people would say that zazen is a difficult practice and Pure Land nenbutsu practice is easier. Actually, when I felt compelled to chant *Namu Kanzeon Bosatsu* when I was eking out a living making charcoal in the mountains of Shimane Prefecture, there was no way I could do zazen in those difficult circumstances. In the end, for me shikantaza and chanting practice were not different things but were one and the same faith-based practice powered by my own life energy.

When we are able to do zazen, we should do it; when we are able to chant wholeheartedly, we should do that. My aim is to receive the Buddha's message whether I'm using either an elegant stereo system or a handheld transistor radio. What does faith mean when doing zazen or chanting wholeheartedly? It just means doing zazen correctly or chanting correctly. Correct zazen means that, when we sit, we entrust ourselves to zazen. And when we chant wholeheartedly, we entrust ourselves to chanting. We shouldn't use our own egotistical ideas to try to assure ourselves about the purpose of our zazen, aiming for a satori experience. It's the same with chanting. We should not invoke the name and spoil it with our own selfish dualistic thoughts. We shouldn't think that chanting will free us from suffering[92] or that we are definitely heading for the Pure Land paradise.

How much value do you attach to your own ideas? You might think that zazen is not real zazen unless your mind is perfectly clear, and you feel good when sitting. Or you might be dissatisfied chanting the nenbutsu unless you experience freeing yourself from suffering or being reborn in the Pure Land. We place too much value on these experiences, which are nothing more than shabby thoughts that recur and persist: "This is really good zazen" or "Now I am really chanting correctly."

92. "All will be freed from suffering" appears in the Kannon-gyo where the Buddha explains that by wholeheartedly calling out the name of Avalokiteshvara—that is, Kannon—all will be freed from suffering.

Of course, this is not entrusting ourselves to zazen or chanting; in the end, this is not true zazen or chanting the name of Amida or Kanzeon. The zazen of Dogen or the nenbutsu of Shinran has nothing to do with our own perceptions or the ludicrous thoughts that flash into our minds. Delusory thoughts that pop into the minds of us ordinary people don't amount to much. We don't need to get caught up in them. Throughout our lives, no matter how many sad times and happy times there are, by getting past these mountains and rivers—I can't tell you how—when there is no longer anything left to say, there's some small light at the end of the tunnel. As I said before, we derive the power of our life and engage in true religion, sitting motionless in zazen or chanting the nenbutsu.

In *Gakudoyojinshu* (Advice on Studying the Way), Dogen uses the phrase, "practicing within delusion."[93] This doesn't mean zazen practice after delusion has been averted, nor does it mean zazen practice in which we deliberately incline ourselves toward delusion. We just practice in delusion, encountering delusions from all directions. Our reality is always that thoughts of gain and loss, love and hate, keep coming and going in our mind. We nevertheless practice in the midst of our delusions, manifesting the true form of the undefiled self with the undefiled form that is nothing more than zazen. We can say that is the reality of the true form of the self of the Buddha. In other words, that is the Buddha that practices within delusion. Concerning this Practice Buddha, Dogen says,

> All buddhas without exception fully practice dignified conduct: this [practice] is Practice Buddha. Practice Buddha is neither a reward-body buddha nor a transformation-body buddha; neither a self-nature-body buddha nor an other-nature-body buddha. [This Buddha] is neither gradual awakening nor original awakening;

93. "To practice within delusion" is an expression found in Dogen's *Gakudoyojinshu*, which he wrote shortly after returning to Japan from China.

> neither by-nature awakening nor no-awakening. Buddhas like these cannot stand shoulder-to-shoulder with Practice Buddha. We should know that all buddhas in the buddha way do not wait for awakening.[94]

You see, even if we don't perceive it, when practicing in the midst of delusion we are actualizing the Buddha practicing within delusion. Dogen further says,

> When you look at the dignified conduct of Practice Buddha, do not use the eyes of heavenly beings or human beings; do not use the heavenly and human sentiments. Do not try to measure [dignified conduct] with them. Even those in the ten stages of the sage and three stages of the wise have not yet known or clarified it, much less can human or heavenly beings fathom them.

There was once a Pure Land devotee by the name of Genshichi Santa. From a young age, he had wished to attain peace of mind. He traveled far and wide, seeking guidance in his quest for understanding. He met with other Pure Land devotees and asked them about the Way. He roamed all the way from Tamba to the Tokai region of Honshu[95] and on the evening of December 30, 1862, he reached the village of Nodamura in Mikawa Province and visited a man named Wahei-san.[96]

In the eyes of the sincere devotee Genshichi, there was no New Year's

94. This and the following quotation are taken from *Shobogenzo Gyobutsu Iigi* ("The Dignified Conduct of Practice Buddha"). I have included more of the original text than did Uchiyama Roshi so that the reader can get a fuller picture of Practice Buddha. Unpublished translations by Shohaku Okumura.

95. Tamba is in the northern Kansai area. The Tokai region is on the main island of Honshu and includes Aichi, Shizuoka, Mie, and southern Gifu prefectures.

96. At this period in Japanese history, only samurai and aristocrats were allowed to have family names; hence this man was known only by his first name, Wahei-san.

holiday.[97] At that time, Wahei-san was over seventy years of age. Furthermore, Wahei-san was bedridden in the final stages of a grave disease and would die three days later on January 2. He was just skin and bones, more dead than alive. When Genshichi saw Wahei-san's emaciated body he was deeply moved, but he quickly asked him,

> I would like to humbly ask you. I suffer from doubts about the afterlife, and I have come to receive your nourishing spiritual advice. I suppose judging by your appearance it appears that this terrible illness must surely be causing you a great deal of suffering. If you think about your having come to this, with no possibility of recovery, is the future bright for you or dark for you?

Wahei-san smiled and said,

> Is the afterlife bright? No, it is not bright. Is it dark? No, it is not dark. Right now, the only thing that I am concerned about is the suffering caused by my illness. If I must determine if things are light or dark, then Amida wouldn't exist.[98] *Namu Amida Butsu*, *Namu Amida Butsu*.

Then Seishiro-san, who was showing Genshichi around, asked Wahei-san a question: "When you chanted the nenbutsu just now, in the midst of your grave illness, were you contemplating Amida's benevolent compassion?" Then the gravely ill Wahei-san strained to raise his voice and said, "Seishiro-san, Seishiro-san, because I have heard that it is Amida Buddha's work to lead us to the Pure Land, I don't need to worry about

97. In Japan, New Year's is the most important holiday. Traditionally, families reunite and all work is stopped for several days to celebrate the New Year. However, Genshichi was such a serious Way seeker that the New Year's holiday did not matter to him.

98. In other words, "It is not up to me to judge if the future is light or dark for me. I just have faith in Amida's vow to save all beings."

my own condition."[99] Then Seishiro-san said, "All right, sometimes I feel I understand but at other times I don't really understand this expression *tanomu ichinen*.[100] Can you give me a clear explanation of this expression?" Wahei-san replied,

> You are right, you are right. It is said that we ordinary human beings cannot understand this expression. Even Rev. Rennyo said that he could not understand.[101] Why didn't he understand? Rennyo transmitted the teaching just as it had been transmitted to him. That is to say, Rennyo never published his personal explanation of the expression, *tanomu ichinen*. He transmitted the teaching just as it is by saying, "*Namu* means taking refuge or giving thanks" or "If you just rely on Amida Butsu . . ." It is impossible for us ordinary beings to comprehend what Amida offers us. So, if we think that we understand what is meant by *tanomu ichinen*, then our rebirth in the Pure Land is not settled. When we feel like the more we listen, the more we cannot understand, that is all the more reason why our rebirth in the Pure Land is certain. This is what we should understand. We need to hear the teaching in this way.[102]

I am particularly moved by Wahei-san's attitude toward chanting the nenbutsu. His faith in Amida's vow was such that he sat immoveable like

99. Wahei-san is saying that he can just trust in Amida's vow to lead all beings to the Pure Land.

100. This is a common Pure Land expression, meaning that the practitioner relies on the saving power of Amida Buddha's other-power with wholehearted faith in Amida's vow in one thought-moment.

101. Reverend Rennyo (1415–1499) was the eighth head priest of Honganji Temple in a line from Shinran. He is revered as the "second founder" of the Jodo Shinshu tradition. He translated Shinran's teachings into simpler language and organized the Shinshu movement into a coherent structure.

102. According to Uchiyama Roshi, this is from a work titled *The Tale of the Old Man Santa*. Unfortunately, nothing else is known about this work.

a huge boulder, not questioning or trying to comprehend whether the afterlife is light or dark or whether he understood Amida's work or not, or whether he should take refuge in Amida's vow.[103]

I would like to offer the following poem:

> Even though I don't sense or know it myself that wholeheart-
> edly chanting the name is wholeheartedly chanting the name,
> I practice wholeheartedly chanting the name.

The monk and poet Ryokan composed the following poem. I hope to appreciate its profound meaning.

> Although there is nothing I can actually touch [to make sure],
> I trust in the way of the Dharma because it's just as it is.

In the Pure Land tradition, the nenbutsu is the working of Amida Buddha that prompts us to awaken to the great reality of great compassion. It is not in saying or chanting the name that we awaken to the greater reality; rather, that greater reality prompts us to awaken to a world beyond the ego self. The individual then responds in gratitude by saying *Namu Amida Butsu*. The key point is that the recitation of the nenbutsu is not the condition for birth in the Pure Land; the condition has already been settled by Amida Buddha.

103. In other words, he put his own personal doubts aside and simply had faith in Amida Buddha's vow.

14. The Scenery of My Life
The Seven Disasters and Three Poisons[104]

Continuing, I'd like to consider the meaning of each of the words that make up *Kanzeon—world* (世を), *perceives* (観ずる), and *sound* (音)[105]—and the various phrases that appear in the opening question-and-answer section of the sutra. The phrases are "all beings experiencing suffering and agony"; "all of them would be freed"; and "chant with one mind." I would like to look at and apply their religious meanings to my discussion of the Kannon-gyo.

First, the seven disasters: fire, flood, encountering ogre demons, being attacked physically, being tormented by satyrs and ogres, being bound in shackles and chains, and facing vengeful thieves. The sutra says if we wholeheartedly call out the name of the bodhisattva then we will be freed from these sufferings.

Next is the section on the three poisons—lust, anger, and stupidity: "If any living beings are afflicted with a great deal of lust . . . have a great

104. The seven troubles, disasters, or misfortunes presented in chapter 25 of the Lotus Sutra are (1) fire; (2) water or floods; (3) ogres; (4) the ruler; (5) demons; (6) torments with cangues, a punishment similar to stocks or pillories; and (7) bandits. Chanting the name of Kanzeon Bosatsu will save one from these disasters. The three poisons are the three major evil passions defined in Buddhism: hatred, anger, or aggression; desire, covetousness, greed, or attachments; and stupidity or ignorance.

105. *Kanzeon* is written 観世音, with the characters for "perceive," "world," and "sound," respectively. Uchiyama Roshi chooses to interpret this as the "sound that perceives the world."

deal of anger and rage . . . or are deluded by great folly [stupidity], if they always keep in mind and revere Perceiver of the Cries of the World Bodhisattva [Kanzeon], they will be separated from the three poisons."[106]

The next section in the sutra concerns the two desires of human beings. In this case, if they are seeking a male child or a female child, if they pray to Kanzeon Bosatsu and make offerings, then they will bear a son blessed with merit, virtue, and wisdom. If they want a daughter, then they will bear one marked with beauty and virtue and who will come to be respected by all.

This encompasses the entire question-and-answer section found at the beginning of the Kanzeon chapter of the Lotus Sutra. (See the diagram on page 33.)

According to an ancient commentary on the separate answers section, chanting the name of Kanzeon when encountering the seven disasters is termed "corresponding to speech." In the three poisons section, "always mindful and venerate" corresponds to thought. In the two desires section, "making prostrations and offerings" corresponds to the body. In other words, as is commonly said, the combination of body, speech, and thought are the three sources of karma.[107] I suppose one could interpret it in this way, but if we don't bother with this old commentary, if we read the Kannon-gyo just as it is, especially if we look at the grouping together of these three sources of karma (actions, speech, and thought), I feel that it is too formal and even seems unnatural to me. This is because the Kannon-gyo, more than anything, is the true form of the self, and we need to take it as a matter of course that when reading and chanting the sutra from the standpoint of the Buddhadharma, we are actualizing the true form of the self. As long as we understand that chanting the sutra manifests the self, so chanting (speech) and being always mindful and

106. Reeves, *Lotus Sutra*, 372.

107. This phrase can be translated as "the three sources of karma" or "the three categories of karma": deeds, words, and thought.

venerating Kanzeon and making prostrations and offerings (body) are never separate from each other. Aren't these three just a single expression of our faith in one mind? Also, aren't the seven disasters, the three poisons, and the two desires just different aspects of the same thing—namely, "countless living beings experiencing suffering and agony"?[108] And being released from the three poisons and the desire for worldly pleasure, don't these all constitute one thing—namely, "being freed from suffering"? In any case, I think that it's okay to have this alternative interpretation of these expressions. Without separating body, speech, and mind into three separate entities, but rather looking at their connectedness, I would like to appreciate this ancient commentary from a different point of view.

Earlier, when I mentioned the meaning of the sufferings in the question-and-answer portion at the beginning of the sutra, I spoke about suffering as the "suffering in an unobstructed view of life." Indeed, I thought that this essential suffering of our entire life is what the sutra refers to in the question-and-answer part. Therefore, I wanted to ask how all human beings can escape from this basic condition of suffering.

However, when we look at the various sufferings found in the separate answers section of the sutra, it is not useful for understanding the broader category of "suffering as seen from an unobstructed view of life." Why not? Because the sufferings described there are only the specific and incomplete sufferings of a single individual, particularly the sufferings of the seven disasters. It is more useful to think of the seven disasters as an iteration of the polluting thoughts of the three poisons of greed or lust, hatred or anger, and delusion or ignorance. What does each of the seven disasters really mean? It is easier to look at them if we think about how the three poisons operate.

The three poisons form the basis of all delusions harming all beings, like a poisonous snake or dragon—so they are named the three poisons.

108. This and the next sentence refer to the first part of the Kannon-gyo, in which living beings are freed from their suffering by calling out the name of Kanzeon Bosatsu.

According to the *Dazhidu lun*,

> We have greed and cling to the people who benefit us, and we have anger (hatred) for the people who are against us.
> These afflictions do not arise from wisdom but from mental confusion.
> Therefore, it is called ignorance.
> These three poisons are the roots of all delusions.[109]

Our minds are always wandering all over the place, choosing between this and that, and loving this and hating that. In that frame of mind, the face of attachment and sexual passion is manifest in the term *lust*. The face of loathing and hate is manifest in the term *wrath*. And the feeling of living in a constant state of turmoil is captured in the term ignorance. As the "Xinxinming" says, "The Great Way is not difficult for those who do not choose." However, because we are attached to choosing (based on wrath and greed), we encounter all sorts of difficulties and continue a journey through endless night. This is ignorance. For example, perhaps you were to say something like this: "If you say that I should separate myself from the world of passion, I would be lonely and unable to do this." Or perhaps this: "If you say that I should not have likes and hates and not indulge in competition with others," then you are not talking about just lust and anger, but one's view of life layered over by ignorance.

Once I accompanied my teacher, Sawaki Roshi, to a temple where he gave a talk. After his lecture, the mother of the temple priest came over to me and spoke in a soft voice: "Roshi's talk today was wonderful. Indeed, I'm sure that my daughter-in-law's ears were burning." Later, the daughter-in-law (the wife of the temple priest) came over and whispered to me, "What a wonderful talk today. I'm sure my mother-in-law's ears

109. Unpublished translation by Shohaku Okumura.

were burning. A truly wonderful talk!" Well, even if we agree that it was a wonderful talk, which woman do we believe? In any case, these women did not understand the talk as an opportunity to deepen their understanding of the Buddhadharma. Instead, both saw the talk as a weapon to attack the other person. It just showed the complete depth of their ignorance.

But ignorance isn't a problem that only ordinary people have. We also need to look at the motives behind forging ahead with the highest level of scientific research that our human culture produces. Isn't it often linked to an arms race? Looking at the world of humans, we can only think that this is rooted in our deep-seated greed and anger. If it is considered a glorification of the purity of our human civilization, then I can only let out a deep sigh, lamenting the misguided ignorance of human beings.

It is often said, "The root cause of the three poisons is worldly desire." Indeed, it is these three poisons that create the ups and downs in our lives, producing complications and dissension. Ultimately, we strangle ourselves and inevitably push ourselves against a wall. For sure, the suffering caused by the various aspects of the three poisons is set forth in the seven disasters section of the sutra.

I once recommended to someone that they read the sutra, but when I met them again, they said, "The Kannon-gyo was so silly that I couldn't take it seriously. I read 'If anyone who embraces the name of Perceiver of the Cries of the World Bodhisattva falls into a great fire, the fire will not burn that person'[110]—but this is ridiculous!" But that person wasn't able to understand the meaning of *fire* as anything except something that burns you, so my recommendation that this person read the sutra was not helpful.

After perusing many books on the mystical virtue of the Kannon-gyo, I found the following story:

110. Reeves, *Lotus Sutra*, 371.

> On a very windy day, a fire started near my house and my house was in its path. I was very upset, and I started to clear loads out of my house. At some point, I went into a dreamlike state and started chanting *Namu Kanzeon Bosatsu, Namu Kanzeon Bosatsu*. Then what happened? Suddenly, the direction of the wind changed, and the fire veered away and burned another house, but my house was saved. I was shocked and surprised by this clear manifestation of Kanzeon's grace, and I became a faithful believer.

Well, if this story had appeared in a comic book, that would be one thing. But it is in fact recorded in a book about religion as a true story of faith.[111] What an odd and shallow point of view—"Your house can burn down, that's fine, as long as my house is spared. I'm very grateful!" If we understand the word *fire* in the Kannon-gyo as merely something that burns us, and then call the sutra "ridiculous" (like the first person), or we believe that Kanzeon's grace is something to be grateful for (like the second person)—well, we are missing the point entirely.

The four modes of interpretation[112] have existed since ancient times and differentiate four ways to interpret sutras. For example, the word *fire* does not mean literal fire. Instead, we must look for the deeper meaning behind the word. It is written in the *Kannongisho*[113] that "There are many kinds of fires, such as the fire of karmic retribution, the fire of karma, or the fire of delusive desires." Also, various Buddhist sutras say, "We should

111. I have been unable to find any information about this book that Uchiyama Roshi refers to.

112. *Shishaku* refers to the four methods used to interpret words or phrases in Buddhist sutras. These four methods differ somewhat according to the particular Buddhist sect. Here, Uchiyama Roshi is probably referring to the fourth method found in Tiantai analysis, particularly expounded by Zhiyi. The fourth method can be translated as "to explain a phrase in such a way as to perceive the ultimate truth of all things with mind."

113. The *Kannongisho* (観音義疏) by Tiantai Zhiyi is a comprehensive commentary on the Kannon-gyo. He also wrote another well-known commentary titled *Kannongengi* (観音玄義), which focuses more on the religious meaning of the text.

also contemplate that the fire of impermanence burns the innumerable worlds and immediately seek to save ourselves." Or "The angry mind is fiercer than a raging fire." Or "Even if we are born in the rapturous seventh heaven, the fire is still burning above our heads." In other words, if the fire of impermanence consumes our entire existence, then this fire of delusion also burns up the positive things in our lives. Also, I would say that clinging to the thought "I'm enlightened" is another way of being consumed by fire.

In another passage in the *Kannongisho* commentary, we find the following:

> The myriad bodies of dwellers in *avici* hell[114] are completely burned from top to bottom, and smoke from fires rises from the homes of the hungry ghosts[115] and burns their entire bodies. Animals are cooked in boiling hot water. *Asuras*[116] also have fire calamities. Also, we witness actual fires in the human world.

The *avici* hell, *pretas* or hungry ghosts, animals, asuras, and human beings mentioned in this commentary are called the five paths[117] in Buddhism, and each of these evolve from the three poisons that affect our minds. Therefore, we can understand this so-called great fire described in the five paths as essentially an aspect of the three poisons manifesting in the circumstances and situations in our lives. In the ultimate competition

114. Avici hell is the destination of beings who have committed the most heinous acts: patricide, matricide, wounding a buddha, or causing a schism in the sangha. Beings reborn in this hell are constantly burned alive in hot flames.

115. Pretas, or hungry ghosts, are born into this unfortunate condition as a result of greed and avarice in a previous life.

116. Asuras are mythical beings described as constantly engaged in futile warfare with the gods above them to regain access to their lost heavenly realm.

117. The five paths mentioned by Uchiyama Roshi are hell, the realm of the pretas or hungry ghosts, animals, humans, and asuras. Buddhist philosophy also traditionally includes a sixth path, that of gods.

between cultures and civilizations, when we bring up the subject of the atomic bomb, its fire is no exception. If we think of this as the consequence of the effect of the three poisons on our minds, we are forced to come to an obvious and deep understanding of what is meant by this sutra.

The other day I read a book by Robert Jungk,[118] *Brighter Than a Thousand Suns: A Personal History of the Atomic Scientists*, about the whole story of the making of the first nuclear weapons. It made a deep impression on me, which I'll never forget.

In 1945, when I heard about the frightful atomic bombs dropped on Hiroshima and Nagasaki, as we Japanese were shuddering with fear, I wondered what kind of people could have created this accursed thing, and what were they thinking and feeling? I thought that this was surely the work of some fiend that had no blood flowing in its veins, so I was interested in reading about what I thought must have been the work of a demon. Of course, I didn't actually think that the bomb was invented by nonhumans. I knew it must have been created by a team of atomic scientists using the latest scientific research. But having said that, why would the scientists create such appalling weapons that risked blowing up all of humankind? In my incomplete understanding, I wondered if these scientists lacked good sense or were beset by anxiety and dread. But in the book titled *The Father of the A-Bomb*, Robert Oppenheimer, the head of the Manhattan Project,[119] provided an answer to my question:

> When you see something that is technically sweet, you go ahead and do it and you argue about what to do about it only after you

118. Robert Jungk (1913–94), an Austrian writer and journalist who wrote mostly on issues relating to nuclear weapons. *Brighter Than a Thousand Suns: A Personal History of the Atomic Scientists* was the first published account of the Manhattan Project and the German atomic bomb project. Jungk was also a futurist and among the pioneers of the international anti-nuclear and environmental movement in the early 1970s.

119. Robert Oppenheimer led the Manhattan Project to create the atomic bomb. Later he had second thoughts about what he and his fellow scientists had created.

have had your technical success. That is the way it was with the atomic bomb.[120]

Further, Carl Freidrich von Weizsäcker[121] said that they were like children playing with fire, and before they knew it, the flames flared up. I understood that the thinking of the top-notch atomic researchers who studied the technical issues surrounding the bomb was summarized by Weizsäcker's remarks. Using difficult words to describe research or technology and using formulas that the uninitiated layperson cannot understand, these brilliant scientists were able to perform calculations that make difficult cosmological principles clear. However, as ordinary people, we must ask with much trepidation, who in the world are these people? I asked myself if these researchers lacked any moral compass. They seem like evil, delinquent children engaged in a senseless act of violence, like they thought it would be fun to detonate some dynamite in a small house.

Furthermore, they also possessed an insatiable desire for fame, political power, and authority. Greed and jealousy jumbled together with the ambitions of politicians and the military-industrial complex. Of course, they are just like the delinquent child drenched in the three poisons. Are these ill-natured-yet-brilliant idiots under the influence of the three poisons going to bring about another huge conflagration with atomic and hydrogen bombs?

To truly understand what we are doing every day—regardless of the scale of our activities or which organization we belong to or what kind

120. "J. Robert Oppenheimer" in Susan Ratcliffe, ed., Oxford Essential Quotations, online edition (Oxford University Press, 2016).

121. A German physicist and philosopher. He performed nuclear research in Germany during the Second World War under the leadership of Werner Heisenberg. He joined the German nuclear energy project participating in efforts to construct an atomic bomb. However, it is debatable whether he and other German scientists worked seriously to construct a German atomic bomb.

of clever technology we are involved with—we are only busily rushing around in the world of the three poisons. I believe that it would be beneficial for us to make it a habit to read a sutra with a calm mind at least once a day.

I have explained the meaning of the fire disaster, so what about the water disaster, or the demon disaster, or all the other disasters? I would like you to calmly contemplate and appreciate each of these seven disasters in your own way. The seven disasters are in the end nothing more than the condition of our lives when we are captured by the three poisons. This is only the scenery of our life. If we continue to appreciate the sutras firsthand, how much will we benefit from this truth? Because, actually, Bodhisattva Inexhaustible Mind[122] is none other than us.

122. Bodhisattva Inexhaustible Mind appears at the beginning of the Kannon-gyo and asks the Buddha the question that begins the sutra.

15. The Difficulty of Maintaining Bodhisattva Vows

Regarding the Two Basic Human Desires[123]

I have asked you to bear with me when I told personal stories, and I hope that you don't mind if I tell one more. It is a from my past, about the early days of my second marriage.[124]

About a year after we were married, my wife became pregnant. When she said, "I think that I may be pregnant," it didn't feel like it was really happening to us. It seemed somehow unreal to me.

Before long, after the doctor examined my wife and confirmed that she was indeed pregnant, her belly began to swell, and she started using an *iwata obi*.[125] We talked, as couples do, about the baby and started to show concern for the new life that was on the way. One evening I asked my wife, "So how do you think that we should design our baby?" In those days, I wasn't really working so I was sitting around reading baby books and spending my days building my loving relationship with my wife. In response to my odd question, my wife made a strange face. Since

123. As stated previously, the two basic human desires are for worldly pleasures and a long life.

124. Uchiyama Roshi was married three times. His first wife died of tuberculosis. As he describes here, his second wife died from complications during pregnancy. He married his third wife after he retired as abbot of Antaiji Temple.

125. Traditionally, a belt that is used for back support during pregnancy.

our personalities were similar, she said, "So you want to design the baby, huh?" I said, "Okay, let's create a blueprint for the baby. It is important for people to create a deliberate plan." I grabbed paper and pen and started writing, giving our plan the title, *Synopsis of the Plan for Our Beloved Child*, and looked over at my wife. With a pleased expression on her face, she said, "I think that a light complexion would be the best." I replied, "Well, wheat color is a modern color and is not bad, and since both you and I are not that dark, more than likely our child will be born with a light complexion." So, I wrote down on the paper: "No. 1. Color: White."

Next, I pleased my wife by saying, "Of course it would be okay if the baby's eyes and nose resemble mine, but since your nose is charming and cute, let's use yours." I wrote down: "No. 2. Eyes and Nose should resemble Chizuko." Next, we continued designing the mouth, the shape of the face, the height, and so on. During this discussion, my wife said, "It's best if the baby has a healthy and robust body, but since neither of us is very healthy, that's a problem." To which I responded, "Yes, of course it's best if the child is healthy. All we can do is make sure that you eat nutritious foods to build up your body. But do we intend to give birth to a boy or girl?" To which she responded, "I really don't know." I said, "Well, since we don't know for sure, we don't know if we can implement our design. Anyway, either a boy or a girl is fine. However, I wouldn't like to raise a child who always goes after money." Then I added, "Of course! It would be better if the child were spiritual." My wife agreed. Being a young couple who did not really understand the meaning of our existence, living as if in a dream, we wrote down our plan, without any objection from either of us, that our child would not have money as part of his or her destiny.

Then I said to my wife, "My mother told me that when she was pregnant with me, she always read the Kannon-gyo, so I think that it would be a good idea if you read it, too. This kind of prenatal care is also important.

If you read *The Life of an Amorous Man*,[126] then you might give birth to that kind of child. But if you read the Kannon-gyo, whether it's a boy or a girl, it will be a good child." When I related what fragmentary knowledge about the Kannon-gyo I had learned from my mother, my wife, who was gentle and meek, readily agreed. She began to read the Kannon-gyo during the day and evening. I also bought her a copy of Arai Sekizen's[127] commentary on the Kannon-gyo and she began reading it.

The Kannon-gyo includes the following passage: "If a woman wants to have a son and worships and makes offerings to Perceiver of the Cries of the World Bodhisattva, she will bear a son blessed with merit, virtue, and wisdom. If she wants a daughter, she will bear one marked with beauty, one who had long before planted roots of virtue and will come to be cherished and respected by all."[128] If that were true, then we should have had a truly wonderful child. But despite my wife's efforts, it didn't work out that way. At nearly the last month of pregnancy, my wife suffered from severe morning sickness, which weakened her heart and lead to a heart attack. She suffered all through the night and died the afternoon of the next day. The child died in its mother's body before it could be born. After that, I came to feel that that passage from the Kannon-gyo was nothing but a lie.

However, my wife's death became a turning point in my life. I left home and became a monk. When I consider that I gave my body over to Buddhist practice for approximately the next twenty years, I have come to have a different understanding of this passage. The passage says, basically, that if you make offerings and worship Kannon, a good child will be born. It doesn't mean that we can rely on Kannon to supersede human biology or physiology. That would be a mistake and just an extension of

126. The first novel by Iharu Saikaku (1642–93). Saikaku was a poet and novelist who wrote racy novels about the hero, Yonosuke, and his adventures in the pleasure quarters.

127. Arai Sekizen (1865–1927) was a prominent Soto Zen monk. Though I couldn't find a reference in his biography, he must have written a commentary on the Kannon-gyo.

128. Reeves, *Lotus Sutra*, 372–73.

the three poisons—that is, deluded thinking. We can't rely on this sutra passage to bring about a good birth.

For a pregnant woman, I'm sure that any obstetrician would recommend tranquilly reading sutras, cleaning a Buddhist altar, praying, and offering flowers and pure water rather than reading gruesome detective stories or lurid romance novels. However, this kind of discussion about health and hygiene has nothing to do with Buddhism. Buddhism does not offer medical advice or prescriptions for good health. My wife's case shows this clearly enough: despite her reading and chanting the Kannon-gyo, both she and our poor child died. Buddhism does not offer a specific solution for our life problems. When we look at this passage about the two basic human desires, we need to look at it in an entirely different way. What does the sutra mean about "seeking to give birth to a good child"?

As Dogen says, "To study the Buddha Way is to study the self."[129] Our practice is nothing more than learning about the self. However, when we say, "the self," we usually think this means "me" or "I," but this self that Dogen refers to doesn't mean one's individual self. As far as Buddhism is concerned, this self that we ordinarily think of as "me" is referred to with the expression, "karmic attributes and karmic consciousness."[130] Our lives are a continuation of our past actions, the result of being born into the circumstances created by our society, being raised according to the historical precedents of that society, being schooled according to the current educational trends, the chance experiences we have had up until now, the seasonal weather patterns, the results of our diet, our physique, and the ideas that we have grown up with. These are the results of our accumulated past karma—that is, karmic attributes and karmic consciousness. This is the me that I think of as my own self.

129. Okumura, *Realizing Genjōkōan*, 75.

130. Karmic attributes and karmic consciousness refer to being pulled by karma or self-centeredness. However, someone who has taken the bodhisattva vows is said to be living to fulfill their vows, not for self-centered reasons. For more detail, see Shohaku Okumura, *Living by Vow* (Somerville, MA: Wisdom Publications, 2021), 58.

Dogen Zenji was not thinking about the old Yogacara terms, karmic attributes and karmic consciousness—along with the rest of the Yogacara system of eight consciousnesses—when he wrote, "To study the Buddha Way is to study the self." Rather, Dogen meant to refer to the self that is cut off from and not contaminated by the past—it is just that original self, pure and undefiled. Indeed, to study this self is to study the Buddha Way.

Well, what does *study* mean? In Japanese, the actual meaning of the word for study or learning, *narau*, is "to become one with." In Western philosophy and science, the subject comes first, and we must proceed based on the knowledge of this subject. In the East, the study of wisdom does not require an association with a subject, because it means "to be one with." For example, in learning horseback riding, one must become one with the horse's body and mind, with no separation between the rider on the saddle and the horse under the saddle. This is what one aims for when learning how to ride a horse. Of course, I don't mean to say that in the West this type of learning doesn't exist at all. But Westerners, rather than "becoming one with" are more apt to think of studying as knowing, and to organize this knowledge into a rational order, attaching a great deal of importance to the development of this skill. This makes me think about the different ways that Eastern and Western cultures have intersected—at some point I would like to write about the shared cultural histories of the East and West. In any case, if I might be allowed to oversimply, in the West the aim is to know the truth, but in the East the aim is to study and actualize that reality. Let's use this as a provisional conclusion. When we study the Buddha Way and the self, we genuinely actualize the true form of the self; that is our aim. This actualization is of the greatest importance, and it must be stressed in our practice.

Returning to my discussion of the Kannon-gyo, let us consider again the meaning of the phrase, "seeking to give birth to a good child." It doesn't just mean simply giving birth to a child in the biological sense. If we consider the meaning of being born according to the Buddhadharma, shouldn't we say that the aim is "to genuinely actualize the true form of the self?" As far as Buddhism is concerned, to "give birth to a child" surely does not refer to the birth of an actual child; rather, it must mean to "actualize the Buddhadharma." How we practice the Buddha Way and how we actualize the Buddhadharma is the true meaning of the birth of a child according to the Dharma.

To be more specific, our current practice—right here, right now—is actualizing the eternal Buddhadharma. This "I" that is subject to karmic attributes and karmic consciousness is the three worlds as one mind that is realized as the true form of the self. This is exactly what is meant in Buddhism when we talk about seeking and giving birth to a child. In *Shobogenzo Hokke Ten Hokke* ("The Flower of Dharma Turns the Flower of Dharma") Dogen writes,

> In general, at the time of the Dharma-flower, without fail the father is young and the son is old. It is not that the son is not the son, or that the father is not the father. We should just learn that truly the son is old, and the father is young.[131]

In our practice here and now[132] this father who is younger giving birth to this eternal son who is older is the pattern of birth in the sense of the Buddhadharma. Put simply, the fact that we would like our actions hour by hour and moment by moment to be eternity just as it is—this is what seeking a child means in terms of the Buddhadharma. Therefore, we seek

131. Dogen is commenting on a passage found in chapter 15 of the Lotus Sutra, "Springing Up from the Earth": "It is as if a hundred-year-old pointed to a young person and said, 'This is the man who fathered and raised me.'" See Reeves, *Lotus Sutra*, 288–89. Shohaku Okumura explains: "Uchiyama Roshi understands this story in the Lotus Sutra as a metaphor of the reality of our life. Our practice is the father, and the child is the eternal life of the Tathagata. The young father here and now gives birth to the eternal life." In other words, through our practice we give birth to the eternal Buddhadharma.

132. In other words, we must continue to practice and, according to Okumura Roshi, "In our practice here and now, the Buddha's eternal Dharma body is always actualized and indestructible."

to give birth to the true form of all things as they are (ultimate reality), and this is also the reason we take the four bodhisattva vows:

1. Beings are numberless; I vow to save them.
2. Delusions are inexhaustible; I vow to end them.
3. Dharma gates are boundless; I vow to enter them.
4. Buddha's Way is unsurpassable; I vow to become it.

This is also what seeking to give birth to a male child through our individual practice means, and what it means to seek to give birth to a female child who teaches and leads others in our practice. Furthermore, this is what a man of wisdom is, and also what I think is meant by the desire to seek a woman of compassion. The function when the vows and prayers have been actualized is discussed in the second question-and-answer section of the Kannon-gyo as the function of the thirty-three forms of Kannon. However, it has a deep meaning that, here, the two wishes are mentioned together with the seven difficulties and the three poisons, as one of the examples of undergoing various kinds of suffering and anxiety. Why do we wish for the Buddhadharma to appear before our eyes? And why do we seek the true form of the self linked to the suffering of all beings? One might think this is odd, but that is actually exactly what Dogen says in *Shobogenzo Genjokoan*: "That is because when one first seeks the Dharma, one strays far from the boundaries of the Dharma." So even if a person says that they are trying to seek the Buddhadharma, that person can't help but be part of the suffering of all beings as long as those beings are separated from the Dharma. Even if you say that the true form of the self has been manifested or actualized, if you wish to verify it by your practice, as long as one is attached to the self, "one strays far from the boundaries of the Dharma."

Further, in the same way that I foolishly made a plan for the birth of my child, there are people who make a plan for the birth of a child in the Buddhadharma. When you dream "attaining satori will surely feel great," or think to yourself that you are sitting zazen courageously, you have strayed far away from the boundaries of the Dharma, and both the mother and child have already died.[133] You might make such a plan, but it is nothing more than a plan based on your own personal desires, which have nothing to do with the Buddhadharma.

What in the world is this satori that we seek? Without knowing anything, we must begin this journey of a hundred miles by advancing one step at a time. However, this applies not only to one's own practice, but it is also true of the altruistic vows of a bodhisattva. Without a doubt, it is our obligation to give birth to the Buddhadharma, and it is our anxiety about giving birth to some kind of child—that is, the result of our efforts—that gives rise to the heavy feeling that we are not yet finished.

Dogen described this in *Bendowa*:

> Later I went to Song China and visited various masters in Zhejiang Province, where I learned the ways of the five schools of Zen. Finally, I met Zen Master Rujing[134] on Mount Taipai and completely clarified the great matter of lifelong practice. After that, I returned home in the first year of Sheting (1227). To spread this Dharma and to free living beings became my vow. I felt as if a heavy burden had been placed on my shoulders. In spite of that, I set aside my vow to propagate this, in order to wait for conditions under which it could flourish.[135]

133. That is, seeking to relieve suffering by sitting zazen in order to attain some false satori experience kills our practice.

134. Tiantong Rujing, Dogen's teacher in China who transmitted the Soto lineage to him.

135. From *The Wholehearted Way*, 20. After he returned from China, Dogen resided temporarily at Kenninji Temple. Dissatisfied with the practice there, he left and was living in a small temple in Fukakusa when he wrote *Bendowa*. He eventually left Kyoto to establish Eiheiji Temple in Fukui Prefecture.

Truly Dogen's desire "to spread this Dharma and to free living beings"—and to give birth to the Buddhadharma in Japan—must have felt like a heavy burden on his shoulders. However, in order for a bodhisattva to realize their vows and to ignite the fire of the true life of a human being, the bodhisattva must take bold action. When the parents of the world are perplexed by the behavior of their children, work hard for their children, and feel that their lives are meaningful because of their children, this is exactly the same as following the bodhisattva vow.

In any case, the two basic human desires illuminated in the Kannon-gyo do not pertain to physiological birth but instead refer to giving birth to the Buddhadharma. We should certainly strive for this. However, at the same time we should realize that this action is just a manifestation of the suffering of all beings and the seven difficulties and three poisons.

Having considered the sutra's phrase, "all of them will be freed," next I will look at the phrases "wholeheartedly chanting," "always keeping in mind with humble reverence," and "worship and make offerings." I would like to explain how all of them comprise a single attitude of religious faith.

16. Single-Mindedly Chanting the Name of Kanzeon Bosatsu as the House Where We Live

Chanting single-mindedly means chanting with one's whole heart. As I explained in chapters 11 and 12, the sound that flows from chanting comes from the perspective of the priceless one mind of emptiness. Chanting in a loud voice *Namu Kanzeon Bosatsu* and verifying the sound of emptiness with one's own ears is a wonderful thing. Yet I have a feeling that it might just stink a bit of the old established type of Buddhism. This is just my personal opinion, but I think many of us feel alienated from this fossilized Buddhism. As for my own practice, instead of chanting out loud in front of people, I always chant silently in my own mind. Everyone can practice chanting in this way. It would be fun if chanting with one mind were like using a transistor radio to tune in to the voice of the Buddha, or the sound of the true form of the self, or the sound of the universe. Even better would be if shikantaza worked like a hi-fi system to bring us the raw essence of the Buddha ancestors or the actualization of the true form of the self. I would like to interpret this as the "one religious life of the self," whether it is chanting *Namu Kanzeon Bosatsu*, chanting *Namu Amida Butsu*, or sitting shikantaza.

Additionally, the passage about the three poisons says that if someone is afflicted with a great deal of the three poisons,[136] let them keep in mind

136. The three poisons are lust or greed, anger, and ignorance or stupidity.

and revere Avalokiteshvara Bodhisattva and they will be freed.[137] The phrase "always keeping Avalokiteshvara in mind" means to express veneration or respect using forms—for example, a bow or another gesture of veneration using our body—or holding respect or veneration in our mind. In other words, this phrase declares that both gestures and thoughts should be reverent. Therefore, we can use a translation of the Sanskrit term *smṛti* to understand "keeping in mind with humble reverence" as meaning "maintaining mindfulness."[138]

In the end, because the three poisons are a bad habit that we have clung to since the beginningless past, even if we chant the name of Kanzeon only a little bit, that doesn't extinguish the benefit. A cursory reading of the sutra causes us to think that if we always keep the name in mind, we will be freed from the three poisons. However, I wonder if it is truly possible to constantly chant and keep *Namu Kanzeon* in mind. Maybe it would be possible if one could sit quietly all day long with nothing to do. But most people must carry on with their daily activities. If the way to keep the name of Kanzeon in mind is by chanting all day long and neglecting our work, then it would be utterly impossible for anyone to enter the universal gateway. There must be another meaning of "always keeping in mind."

Even if you were able to chant *Namu Kanzeon*, *Namu Kanzeon* silently in your mind for twenty-four hours continuously, I believe that it still wouldn't be in line with the true religious meaning of continuing to keep in mind the name of Kanzeon with reverence. The reason is the word *always*. If you say the flow of time means there are no gaps, then chanting is not about piling up the number of chants. Shinran ridiculed this kind of practice, our futile efforts to fill the time

137. Actually, in the sutra each of the three poisons is mentioned separately.

138. This phrase can be translated as "continuation of mindfulness" or "maintaining mindfulness." An alternative translation perhaps more compatible with shikantaza practice might be "maintaining mindfulness sitting in the zazen posture and letting go of thought."

gaps, as "self-power practice." He felt that we would be exhausted by our efforts and give up.

Stacking instances of maintaining correct mindfulness like piling up sweet dumplings on a large offering platter,[139] being obsessed about not dropping one, using our human effort to dangerously balance and reverently offer up this plate—that's not what is meant by "keeping Kanzeon in mind with humble reverence." Instead, no matter what, we are always producing the sound of our chanting from our mindfulness of the self without defilement. Therefore, whenever or wherever we chant *Namu Kanzeon*, it is precisely for this reason that we must be chanting Kanzeon's name without being defiled by the three poisons. This is truly keeping Kanzeon in mind with humble reverence. But that is not all. It is precisely because we are in the midst of always keeping Kanzeon in mind with humble reverence that only chanting reverently in our minds is not truly chanting Kanzeon's name. When we work, just working each moment right here, right now—that is chanting the name without defilement, using our body, and it is the activity of the immeasurable divine power of Kanzeon. Therefore, always venerating Kanzeon from the standpoint of the true form of the self, discovering the one mind—that is, the reality of life—is indeed the basis of the faith that comes from one mind. Therefore, chanting with one mind is itself keeping Kanzeon's name in mind with humble reverence.

139. *Dango* are sweet dumplings used as offerings in Japanese temples. A large number of these round dumplings are stacked on large plates or trays and set before the various Buddha images as offerings.

The usual Japanese reading of some sentences from the Chinese translation of the Longer Sukhavativyuha Sutra[140] is: "All living beings who hear the name will believe and feel joy and have an ardent wish. If they hope to be born in that land by performing meritorious deeds earnestly, they will be born there." But Shinran famously changed the way to read the Chinese. He read it this way: "All living beings who hear the name will believe and feel joy and have an ardent wish. They hope to be born in that land.[141] [Amida Buddha] has been sending us his merit earnestly. [All living beings] who want to be born in that land will be born there."[142]

In Shinran's interpretation, the subject Amida is inserted in the middle of the sentence as all sentient beings, and while this may make for a forced reading in Chinese, it accords with the important facts of Shinran's personal religious experience: "Amida Buddha has been sincerely sending us his merit." If Shinran didn't read the text in this way, it wouldn't have made sense to him or accorded with his religious experience. At

140. Three Pure Land scriptures are central to the Pure Land school, and especially the Japanese Jodoshu and Jodo Shinshu: (1) the Sukhavativyuha Sutra, or the Larger Sutra on the Buddha of Immeasurable Life, sometimes called the Infinite Life Sutra; (2) the Sutra on the Contemplation of the Buddha of Immeasurable Life; and (3) the Amitabha Sutra, or the Smaller Sutra on the Buddha Amitabha. In the Larger Sutra, the eighteenth vow reads as follows: "All sentient beings, as they hear the name, realize even one thought-moment of faith (*shinjin*) and joy, sincerely direct their merits, and aspire to be born in that land. They then attain birth there." Shinran, however, read the Chinese in the following way: ". . . which is directed to them from Amida's sincere mind . . ." Thus, Shinran was trying to show that Amida Buddha created the path to religious awakening and gives that virtue to sentient beings in the form of the name—that is, *Namu Amida Butsu*.

141. "Land" in this passage refers to the Pure Land of Amida.

142. It centers around the concept of tariki, "other power," in that Shinran asks us to rely on the merit and the grace emanating from Amida's vow to allow all sentient beings to be born in the Pure Land. In other words, we just need to have faith in Amida's vow to attain birth in his land where ideal conditions exist to be released from suffering and attain enlightenment.

that point, we discover ourselves being saved by the power of the voice of Amida's original vow beckoning us. I think Shinran was urging us to use the other-power nenbutsu, saying that we must accept the original vow of Amida just as it is.[143]

Dogen Zenji's practice of enlightenment[144] is exactly the same thing. In *Bendowa*, Dogen says, "Also it was said, 'A person who sees the Way practices the Way.' You should know that you must practice in the midst of attaining the Way."[145] In other words, the true form of the empty self, just as it is, is undefiled practice. Instead of just trying to gain some merit for ourselves to obtain some desired result, we instead continuously practice keeping Kanzeon in mind with humble reverence. By virtue of being nurtured and cared for by one mind—that is, emptiness—we chant here and now as an expression of our reverence and gratitude.

Therefore, it's not about silently chanting one time or ten thousand times or however many times. At the same time, I want you to know that chanting once, right here, right now, just as it is, means always keeping Kanzeon in mind with humble reverence. Further, without tying ourselves down to the feeling that we must recite the name a set number of times, let's just chant the name of Kanzeon whenever we remember or as much as possible, either out loud or silently. When we are suffering, it is perfectly fine to call on a god for help—or when we are sad, bored, ill, unable to sleep, or any other time.

This is indeed the true form of the self, because at this time we return to the true home or resting place of the self.

In *Shobogenzo Raihai Tokuzui* ("Getting the Marrow by Doing Obeisance"), Dogen says,

143. That is, Amida's vow as interpreted by Shinran that "all living beings who want to be born to that land (the Pure Land), will be born there." It is not necessary to acquire merit in order to be born in the Pure Land.

144. In other words, practice and enlightenment are the same thing.

145. From *The Wholehearted Way*, 31.

> Getting the marrow and receiving the dharma always depend upon utmost sincerity and the believing mind. Sincere faith is not something that comes to you from the outside, nor is it something that moves to the outside from within you. It simply signifies prizing the dharma while making light of yourself. It is to flee the world and regard the way as your abode. If you think of yourself as being even only slightly more precious than the dharma, the dharma will not be passed on to you, nor will you attain it.[146]

It is faith that gives importance to the Dharma and living the Way as our home and refuge. When we chant from the emptiness of the true form of the self, that is from our home and refuge; indeed, that is the true meaning of faith. If we do this, as we wander among the three poisons, we may think that the region of these three poisons is our home—but this is complete ignorance. We are always reverently chanting from the true form of the empty self, but at some point, we lose sight of the appearance of this foremost truth. We are in a state of turmoil. When we are in this confused state, our thinking becomes solidified, and we come to view the world of the three poisons as our true home. However, it is not inevitable that we take this realm as our home. If we chant reverently from the true form of the self as our home and refuge, we can return to this true form of the self. This is a direct and total leap into the realm of the Tathagata. As Dogen writes in *Shobogenzo Kesa Kudoku* ("The Merit of the *Kesa*"[147]), "Their present possessions and dwellings are motivated by their past karma and are not genuine. Only taking refuge and venerating Buddhadharma authentically transmitted can be their true place to return for the sake of studying the Buddha Way."

146. *Shobogenzo Raihai Tokuzui* ("Getting the Marrow by Doing Obeisance"), in Stanley Weinstein, trans., "Treasury of the Eye of the True Dharma Book 28," *Dharma Eye* 10 (May 2002): 15–22.

147. Buddhist monastic robes.

Having said this, of course we are always wandering aimlessly in the environs of the three poisons; this fact doesn't change. Our gut feeling is that we are always living with the three poisons. However, living among the three poisons and chanting while always keeping Kanzeon in mind with humble reverence is a completely different path. According to the Kannon-gyo, chanting in order to extinguish the three poisons is not the way to be freed from them. Instead, just chanting without expectations is the way to be freed from the three poisons. In other words, chanting and always keeping Kanzeon in mind with humble reverence, without any expectations, completely frees us from the three poisons. It is not a half-baked practice. Freeing ourselves from the three poisons by carrying out this practice as our home and refuge is indeed the meaning of the words in the sutra. Because this body and mind are always keeping *Namu Kanzeon* in mind, chanting in emptiness, this act of chanting itself is the way to be freed from the three poisons. This "I" is always keeping Kanzeon in mind by way of the emptiness of the true form of the self. The chanting is entirely undefiled by the three poisons. Shikantaza is the same thing: practicing emptiness with the never-sullied true form of the self, just as it is.

If that's the case, then is the matter of the three poisons not completely resolved by always keeping Kanzeon in mind with humble reverence? No, it's not resolved. Practicing keeping Kanzeon in mind with humble reverence is the way to extinguish the three poisons, but it is not the way to be freed from the poisons. I dare say that as long as we are alive, the three poisons will not disappear from our ordinary thinking, and so we need to continually repent by chanting *Namu Kanzeon Bosatsu*.

In our frantic modern world, each of us has become more emotionally unstable and we often don't understand what we should be doing or what the best course of action is in a particular situation. Recently, I was in Tokyo during morning rush hour. I boarded a bus, and a guy who looked like he had it in for me pushed me as he got on the bus. I suddenly thought about whacking him in the face without saying anything, and

I felt a keen pleasure fantasizing about it. Since I was wearing my priest's robes, I didn't do it.

I truly respect all these people who commute every day during this kind of rush hour, enduring these buses and trains with a saintly expression. But behind those impassive expressions, I'm sure, just like me, they must sometimes feel the urge to slug someone. Because people are always suppressing and accumulating these emotions, they become neurotic. These days, we see too many people who get short-circuited by their emotions and become violent. For that reason, in these times we need to clearly define some place to calm down, a home or refuge for the self, a place of emptiness where we are always chanting *Namu Kanzeon Bosatsu* in reverence in the true form of the self, where we do not lose sight of being freed from the three poisons.

Actually, this is the admonition I give to myself.

17. Freedom and the Twelve Links of Dependent Origination[148]

Let's consider again the passage from the sutra, "If a woman wants to have a son and worships and makes offerings to Perceiver of the Cries of the World Bodhisattva, she will bear a child blessed with merit, virtue, and wisdom." As I have explained before, this passage is not actually referring to the birth of a biological child. Interpreted from a Buddhist perspective, "giving birth to a child" means actualizing the Dharma, or actualizing eternity. Furthermore, don't worshiping and keeping in mind and revering all mean praying or making offerings? Let's explore exactly what it means to pray and to make offerings.

When people offer a votive light to illuminate a household Shinto shrine or a Buddhist altar and clap their hands twice or place their hands together in gassho, I don't know if this means that they have faith in the Shinto gods or the Buddha. I think that when they pray and give offerings, they are wishing for safety, good health, or success for themselves and their household. They are not praying or making offerings to a god or Buddha. For the most part, those who think of themselves as believers use prayer as a type of transaction, seeking personal gain, but they are not *truly* praying and making offerings. Unfortunately, they just end up using prayers and offerings with the hope of attaining desires. Compare this to the quiet stillness that pervades the grounds of a Zen temple, with people just practicing Zen

148. In Buddhist philosophy, "dependent origination" refers to how life arises, exists, continues, and ceases. The principle of dependent origination states that all things happen through cause and effect and are interdependent. This could also be translated as the "twelve links of causation."

silently. Zen practice remains totally separate from a wish for household safety or business success. If someone is praying and making offerings with the goal of attaining satori, well, that has nothing to do with enlightenment.

People often say, "I'm not religious. I don't pray or make offerings." I would respond, "Okay, that's fine, that's wonderful. So, what is it that you value? What is it that you revere in your life?" That person might say, "Freedom." I would then say, "You revere your individual freedom, and you dedicate your whole life to the pursuit of your personal happiness. Well, that's wonderful. However, I daresay that if animals could speak, they would sound no different from you—forest animals, wild birds, or even mosquitos. It's just that they cannot speak, so they can't use these words like *freedom* or *happiness*." Have you thought about the true meaning of freedom or happiness? Once I was speaking with a Christian college student when I realized that she was mixing up the freedom written about in the Bible with the word *freedom* that is fashionable these days. I said, "Simply put, this thing called freedom is something that is imposed from the outside—for example, by old customs, by political pressure, or by our neighbors' malicious gossip. Our path in life is necessarily constrained, but not just by these outside powers, but also by our own original natures."

But what does this phrase "our own original nature" really mean? This is the problem. What the Bible means by *freedom* and what society tells us is freedom are two entirely separate things.

Whatever definition of freedom is in vogue, my body, my thoughts, and my desires, all just as they are, constitute "me." Following my body, thoughts, and desires is considered freedom. However, in the Bible, this is not called "our original nature." Rather, it is called "Adam's corpse" or "thoughts of the flesh," and therefore behaving according to one's selfish thoughts is called being a "slave to sin."

> As for you my brothers, you were called to be free. But do not let this physical freedom become an excuse for letting your physical desires control you. Instead, let love make you serve one another.[149]

149. Galatians 5:13.

> Freedom is what we have—Christ has set us free! Stand then as free people, and do not allow yourselves to become slaves again.[150]

In other words, in the Bible, heedlessly acting on my thoughts and desires is termed "being a slave to sin." In contrast, freedom is being set free from the yoke of sin. I cautioned that young lady, "A Christian like you must be able to clearly make this distinction. Otherwise, there will be a huge conflict between what we understand the word *freedom* to mean these days versus what freedom means in the Bible."

Underlying the concept of freedom must be a notion of the self. Usually, we assume we understand the meaning of the word *self*, based only on our ordinary, everyday conceptions of our selves. But a little more reflection shows that we don't really understand the meaning of *self*.

On this point, I think that Shakyamuni Buddha was brilliant. At the onset, Shakyamuni Buddha bade us consider what the source of the self is. Everyone is born from the womb of their mother. However, the Buddha said that it would seem that no one enters the womb through their own self-awareness and volition. In other words, this "self" starts from a state of ignorance, jumps into some mother's womb—this is a cause or condition. (Thinking about this, it's too bad that we didn't choose a niftier womb.) Through "ignorance" and "causation," when we acted without understanding, before we knew it, our self began in this life—that is, consciousness. This provisional self is formed in the mother's womb, and little by little we are endowed with various functions and features and are finally born. And, well, that's the difficult part. Being born is when we show our face in this world. At that time, whether we are male or female has been determined, and our genetic inheritance has been defined by our parents. But at the same time that we show our face in the world, we may be a crown prince or an illegitimate child, Japanese or Jewish, or with birth defects or diseases. People's lives are burdened left and right with such problems, and they often must bear this heavy burden their entire lives. They are made fun of, they feel powerless, or

150. Galatians 5:1.

they are murdered simply for being Jewish, or for simply being Japanese. Though personally you bear no malice against Americans, you may be forced to kill them and then die yourself in the war.

When you show your face in the world, it is not necessarily clear that you will be affected for your entire life by the circumstances of your birth. Rather, if you are brought up in a normal family, as an ordinary person, indeed after you are brought up, I feel that you are allowed to freely choose your own lifestyle and decide according to your own self-awareness and volition. However, after we grow up, are we completely free from constraints or conditions and able to act upon our own volition without being affected by others? We need to consider this point carefully. When we are born into this world, we are subject to a plethora of influences; for example, our environment and circumstances, the surroundings we are brought up in, the education we receive, the influence of our historical era, the situation of our society, the climate of our locality, and the food that we eat. The conditions we encounter after we are born are largely determined by outside circumstances, so our life experiences are also largely determined by such conditions and experiences. Therefore, it is certainly questionable whether our self is truly independent from these influences.

Even so, I don't think that we are necessarily determined that much by outside conditions. Rather, I think and act freely. But here is an interesting point. There was a woman I knew who was always temperamental and got upset easily, causing confusion. Once, when I was talking with her, I thought that she would agree with me when I pointed out, "Your mood seems to change daily according to the weather." She responded with a frosty face, "I don't know what you are talking about. My mood never changes according to the weather, and I don't have mood swings." Wow, I was shocked! I really understood how much her mood was manipulated by outside influences.

The currently postwar fashionable notion of freedom is just the same. A novel written during the Edo period in Japan describes one element of the societal morals of revenge of that time. The book concerns characters who regrettably spend their lives pursuing grudges and feuds. Looking back on them from our point of view, we feel that they wasted their lives. In the same way, in our era of postwar Japan, Japanese people are apt to adopt this word *freedom* without thinking about what it truly means. We use the word *freedom*, mindlessly almost like a mantra. I wonder how future generations will see this? I daresay that probably they will see us as being totally encumbered by this fashionable thought of "freedom" and will either pity us or laugh at us.

In any case, when we feel encumbered by conditions and external coercion, and we feel we are losing our freedom, we are often unaware that we have lost our individual freedom and our ability to think. Then this "I," or indeed anyone, would act from this state of ignorance, and after that it's like our concept of self is just put on an automated conveyor belt. I suggest that we think carefully about this.

In my own experience, I find that I think that I am making personal value judgments and choosing my own direction in life with the intention of being conscious of myself. However, if how I choose my value judgments from the plethora of thoughts in my mind is all determined by my heredity, education, and environment, then that first act of ignorance conclusively determined everything. Moreover, considering my thinking up until now, from this moment the rest of my life is a given. Likewise, I think that we live as a continuance of ignorance followed by the action based on it and continue this as we face old age and death.

Shakyamuni Buddha taught us the twelve links of causation: ignorance, volitional action, conditioned consciousness, name and form, the six senses, sense impressions, feelings, desire or craving, attachment, becoming, birth, and old age and death. Then he taught us about the self. In short, what we usually think of as our self is not solid and fully formed like a hard pickled plum seed is. The Buddha made the following statements:

1. All beings are made by nothing more than conditions that are scraped together. Life comes into existence through dependence on other things or causes.
2. Furthermore, this self, which is unaware and acts, this subject, is just put together randomly and temporarily comes together, so that our actions come about through ignorance.
3. Consequently, my entire life is nothing more than just a random event connected to my ignorance. All things are in flux through the endless circle of birth, death, and rebirth—that is, the circle of transmigration.

This teaching of the twelve links of causation together with the four noble truths form the essential teachings of Shakyamuni Buddha. The more you think about it, this is the essential religious insight of Buddhism and has a very deep meaning. It is not some scholarly intellectual doctrine. I daresay, as long as human beings do not have the scientific skills to create life, I think that they will be unable to establish intellectual proof of Shakyamuni Buddha's insight. However, when one applies this realization to oneself, anyone can see the truth of it. Having said that, no matter how much we try, we cannot entirely comprehend the true profundity of the Buddha's insight. But, based on whatever understanding we have of the Buddha's teaching about the nature of the self, we can abandon the self and take the first step toward religious practice. Truly, knowing that ignorance is only ignorance is taking the first step toward realization.

18. My Mind Is Like the Weather
Taking Refuge and Continually Venerating the Buddhadharma

In the previous chapter, I discussed the twelve links of causation. It is important to understand this basic Buddhist teaching, because when most of us puzzle over what we should do in a particular situation, we believe that we act of our own accord rather than being continuously influenced by the outside world. Because of this, we are ignorant of what is controlling our random actions.

If we are born male, then we think one way; if we are born female, then we think another way. If we are born in Japan, then we think like a Japanese person. If we are born in the twentieth century, then we think like a twentieth-century person. If we are born into an upper-class family, then we think like an upper-class person. If we are born into a lower-class family, then we think like a lower-class person. Each type of person has their own viewpoint. Moreover, they are influenced by the ongoing environment and experiences of their lives, and their viewpoints are determined accordingly. In the end, one comes to understand that thinking is predetermined and that this is exactly what is meant by the method of observation of the self according to the twelve links of causation. In other words, even though we proclaim, "Me, me" in a loud voice, the essence of this self is not really settled at all.

There is an interesting story relating to this in the writings of the Taoist sage Zhuangzi,[151] who writes about the case of Li-Zhen. Li-Zhen was the

151. Brook Ziporyn, trans., *Zhuangzi: The Complete Writings* (Indianapolis: Hackett, 2020), 20.

beautiful daughter of a military man charged with guarding the remote frontier of China. At that time, the king of Chin was looking for the equivalent of "Miss China," and Li-Zhen was presented to him. Having been brought there, whether regrettably or with great joy, one would think that any young girl would believe they were dreaming. However, this wasn't the case for Li-Zhen, who only felt great sadness at being separated from her hometown and her parents, brothers, and sisters. She wept inconsolably until tears drenched her collar. She thought, "What kind of unhappy star was I born under? There has never been anyone in this world who is more pitiable than me," and all those around her felt sorry for her. However, over time she became enamored of the charm of the capital and the elegant palace. The king showered his affections on her, and they lived a life of extravagance together, sharing the king's luxurious bed, feasting on the finest meats and seafood, completely satiated, served by many ladies in waiting. She became used to this life of royalty and, with a joyful expression on her face, said, "Why in the world was I so sad at being separated from that remote frontier backwater? When I think of my life as a country hick, I wouldn't go back. No thank you."

I'm interested in the change of heart that Li-Zhen experienced because of the changing of her measuring stick—that is, the changes between the yardstick she used as a country girl versus the yardstick that she developed as an adult living in luxury. Of course, this was to be expected. Our way of thinking and our actions are simply the results of the habits and modes of thinking that our environment imposes on us. However, Li-Zhen and those like her cannot possibly be aware of this. In any case, as for Li-Zhen, who tells us how satisfied she is with her new life with the king, I believe that every day her heart burns with vanity, her breast ablaze with jealousy and lust. Her good looks will fade, and her life will be consumed by her fear of sickness, old age, and death.

Reading about Li-Zhen's life of royal ease, I am reminded of the life of Shakyamuni Buddha. During the first part of his life, Shakyamuni was exposed to only one way of thinking and the habits of royal life in the palace where he was born. When he realized that he was being stupefied by his life in the palace, he left to become a wandering ascetic. Then, after realizing the twelve links of causation, he was able to return to the true self before all these thoughts and habits. But this is not only possible for Shakyamuni; it is also possible for us. We, too, can break out of the everyday castle of "me, me" and realize that we are pulled around by the persistence of our ignorance and our actions based on it. Because of this, we ourselves must understand the Buddha's twelve links of causation and accept this teaching just as it is, and we must actualize the Buddha's great path to the true self.

Dogen Zenji summarized his insight into the twelve links of causation concisely. In *Shobogenzo Kesa Kudoku* ("The Merit of the *Kesa*"), he says, "Their present possessions and dwellings are motivated by their past karma and are not genuine. Only by taking refuge and venerating Buddhadharma authentically transmitted can their true place of return be for the sake of studying the Buddha Way."[152] These words of Dogen Zenji have deep implications, and we should study, apply, and keep them in mind in our practice day after day and night after night. Where our minds are concerned, all kinds of thoughts are always coming up into our consciousness. But when you are angry or sad or in despair or feeling hopeless, do not lose yourself in the space of a single breath to these thoughts. Instead, I would like you to realize that each of these thoughts is just a result of a measuring stick that was created by your past karmic actions. Tell yourself this in your own mind and do not give in to these feelings and thoughts.

The Chinese poet Hanshan wrote in a poem, "My mind is like the autumn moon." But for a Buddhist practitioner these words are utterly useless. A practitioner must grasp the phrase, "My mind is like the weather." Depending upon the weather, sometimes we feel that our

152. Uchiyama Roshi did not include the second sentence in his quotation from *Shobogenzo Kesa Kudoku* ("The Merit of the *Kesa*"). I added it for further clarification.

mind is like the clear autumn moon. Other times, our mind rages like a powerful tempest; floats like a spring moon; falls like sad, soft autumn rain; is scorched with desire; is made listless by the summer heat; or we lose ourselves in the numbing cold of winter. Like the weather, in each of these instances, our entire bodies and scenery change completely, leaving no trace of the previous forms. This is our mind. We must not take these temporary states so seriously. We must tell ourselves, "I will not trust these passing moods" and "I will not partner with them." Instead, we must tell ourselves, "I will rely on the state before mind." We must actualize exactly this true self. I would like to use the words of Saint Francis Xavier to prove that these teachings of not relying on one's mind and relying instead on the state before mind are not exclusively Buddhist.

Catholicism was first transmitted to Japan when the famous missionary Saint Francis Xavier arrived by sea in 1549. In his diary of his voyage, Francis writes that his ship encountered difficulties. He and his companions lived with constant uncertainty and anxiety about their lives and the success of their mission. They had to overcome countless obstacles and endure danger for many months. Unlike us today, they could not simply relax at a movie theater. When we are in difficult situations, we tend to concentrate our minds on a single point, and we want to grumble to ourselves about it and come to a realization about our predicament.

It seems that Xavier's voyage to Japan was no exception to this kind of pattern. Traveling aboard a Chinese junk from the straits of Malacca to Japan was fine, but the Chinese captain was a superstitious man, and he often consulted his fortune using divination devices. Since he acted on the results of the divinations, he made unwise decisions based on these superstitions. Amid these unfavorable conditions, I wonder if Francis aspired in a saintly way to evangelize to nonbelievers, while enduring so many hardships and dealing with a complaining crew—all without any internal doubts. As a leader in these situations, what did he endeavor to keep in mind? Francis, as the result of his wise insight, summed up his experience: "Our true trust in God is born from not trusting ourselves."

Among those who traveled with Francis, because of the unendingly arduous voyage, some began to be obsessed with various doubts that sprang up in their minds and proliferated, and they forgot that they were on a mission for the sake of God's glory.

Incidentally, these types of problems occur not only on mountain expeditions or when evangelizing nonbelievers. They are also relevant for maintaining good marital relations. When we look at our emotional state, it is clear that in the final analysis we cannot achieve a happy life partnership if we succumb to temporary mood swings. For both the husband and wife, if they are unable to live as saintly men and women, we will see both men and women having extramarital love affairs. Unfaithful thoughts inevitably occur. However, when we consider the "reality" of all these thoughts and how they proliferate, there are endless reasons for bad relations between men and women. In the final analysis, we are unable to understand exactly what is happening. But isn't it that, in the relationship between a man and a woman, trust is born from first not trusting the temptation to cheat on one's partner?

In a similar way, the meaning of making prostrations and offerings to Kannon Bosatsu is precisely manifested in not trusting our temptation to engage in an extramarital affair—ignore such a thought and rely instead on the one mind that comes before the thought of infidelity. This is none other than the sublime one mind that is priceless and undefiled, the one mind that comes before all our petty thoughts and habits. We entrust our bodies and mind to the sound of the universe by taking refuge in the sound that perceives the world, the undefiled practice of chanting the name of Kannon Bosatsu. This is what is meant by making prostrations and offerings to Kannon. Just as I said previously, always keeping Kannon in mind with humble reverence is another name for chanting with one mind.

Certainly, just chanting, "I take refuge in the sound that perceives the world," or "I take refuge in Kanzeon," is also the body carrying out the continuation of ignorant and willful acts that create karma.[153] However, though this is an action, it is not an ordinary act. It is instead the act of giving birth to the Buddhadharma that gives birth to an eternal child.

This is what is meant by the passage in the Kannon-gyo that says, "By making prostrations and offerings to Kannon, a good child—that is, one blessed with merit, virtue, and wisdom—will be born." However, making prostrations and offerings to this one mind is not completed simply in the dichotomy and separation between "one mind that is venerated" (subject) and "the karmic self that venerates" (object). Since the one mind is the true form of the self, this means that in making prostrations to the true form of the self, subject and object become identical and actualize the Buddhadharma. Making prostrations is itself Buddhadharma.

As Dogen says in *Shobogenzo Darani* ("Dharani"), "We should know that making prostrations is the true-dharma-eye-treasury. . . . In general, while making prostrations exists in the world, the buddha-dharma exists in the world; when making prostrations disappears, the buddha-dharma disappears."

In other words, without "making prostrations using this body" or "chanting refuge using this mouth" of this karmic self, the Buddhadharma would be never actualized.

Now, only when making prostrations and offerings mentioned in the Kannon-gyo; that is, chanting *Namu Kanzeon* using this body and this mouth, will Avalokiteshvara manifest.

Dogen quotes the Ancestral Master Nagarjuna in *Shobogenzo Kuyo Shobutsu* ("Making Offerings to Buddhas"):

To seek the fruit of buddhahood,
reciting one praising verse,
chanting one refuge,

153. This refers to the first two of the twelve links of causation, ignorance and willful acts.

burning one pinch of incense,
offering one stalk of a flower:
with small practices like these, without fail, we are able to become
a buddha.

19. The Relaxed and Spacious Life
Traveling the Bodhisattva's World[154]

Any Japanese person knows the venerable priest Bodhidharma, that little toy doll sitting covered with a red mantle.[155] From a very young age, I always liked the Daruma doll. When I was young, my mother would take me to see the head priest at a temple in Kawasaki in Kanagawa Prefecture, just south of Tokyo. Each time, she bought me a little Daruma doll. At that time, I really liked the red color and the friendly rotund body without arms and legs. Later, after becoming a Zen priest, I became a descendant of Bodhidharma. When I began doing zazen, it occurred to me that this was a queer fate. Now I feel completely grateful for this fate, not because I like the red mantle and round body of the Daruma doll, but because I like the focus of this life of mine. Well, actually *like* is not the right word. Even if my life at this moment is strange and miserable, I still think that I can be saved. All I need to do is to resolve to step firmly in the footsteps of this venerable teacher, Bodhidharma, and learn to live as he did.

154. The bodhisattva's world means to live while giving up acting for self-gain. It means living with an attitude of refraining from all fabrication, to be free from the ideas we make up in our head. Uchiyama Roshi called this "opening the hand of thought." In his final address to his students at Antaiji Temple, he said, "Study and practice the buddhadharma only for the sake of the buddhadharma, not for the sake of emotions or worldly ideas" (*Opening the Hand of Thought*, 140). Thus, when we give up acting for self-gain, we travel in the relaxed infinite world of the bodhisattva.

155. In Japan, there is a toy Daruma—Japanese for Bodhidharma—doll as described. When you buy the doll, the irises in both eyes are blank. It is a custom in Japan to make a wish and paint in one iris. When what you are wishing for comes true, then you paint in the other iris.

It is commonly thought that Bodhidharma was a South Indian prince.[156] It is said that he was ordained by Prajnatara and after receiving the precepts and studying the Dharma he traveled by ship, skirting the Indian coast and the Malay peninsula for three years before arriving in China[157] to spread true zazen practice. Stories of the time have him arriving in China during either the Liu Song dynasty (420–479) or Liang dynasty (502–557).

Legend has it that Emperor Wu heard that an eminent monk had arrived from India and he wanted to meet him. From Bodhidharma's perspective, if the emperor truly accepted his Buddhist teachings, then he could use the PR value of this relationship to effectively spread zazen practice in China. In any case, both parties agreed to meet. However, unfortunately both sides seem to have been disappointed with the encounter. The emperor favored the traditional Buddhism that had proliferated in China, and he was a patron of select foreign-born Buddhist monks. But this unkempt monk Bodhidharma didn't fawn over the emperor, and the emperor decided that this kind of person could not be a real monk. As for Bodhidharma, knowing that Buddhism had reached China many years before and that this emperor had appointed many monks to teaching positions, he had a sliver of hope that the emperor might have a good understanding of Buddhism. Instead, the emperor turned out to be a snob who wouldn't assist Bodhidharma's project of spreading zazen in China. For both men, their meeting did not meet their expectations.

So Bodhidharma must have thought, "Well, that's how it is." It had been quite a while since his departure from India and since things hadn't

156. Early accounts of Bodhidharma's life identify him as either Persian Central Asian or South Indian. Here Uchiyama Roshi uses the latter legend. According to recent scholarship, there is scant evidence that Bodhidharma really existed, and many of the stories about him seem to be more like legends than facts. For more detail, see Red Pine, introduction to *The Zen Teaching of Bodhidharma* (New York: North Point Press, 1987).

157. Other stories have Bodhidharma arriving on foot, having traveled over the Himalayas.

been going at all as he had planned, he completely gave up hope for his plans to establish a link with the emperor. Instead, he crossed the Yangtze River, going north to the country of Wei. He chose not to meet the emperor of Wei but went to Shaolin Temple on Mount Song, where he rented a small room in the eastern corridor of the temple and at last started sitting zazen. Though he sat zazen in the corridor, he did not try to recruit others to sit with him. Sitting by himself, this monk from sweltering southern India must have felt cold in northern China, so he covered himself with a red cloak and just sat zazen.

As a matter of fact, Bodhidharma was not challenging the existing Buddhism in China but was simply sitting zazen. If he had sat in the corridor wearing a white headband[158] we would quickly understand that he was looking to call attention to his practice, but since he was just sitting in the temple corridor covering himself with a red cloak, people would wonder why he was sitting there, but no one would know why. In the end, people would just look at him and think that this weird Indian monk was doing a strange thing.

In that case, did Bodhidharma's practice lack direction? No. His practice was focused, and he didn't need to base it on others. Compared to Bodhidharma, people's practice these days depends on being face-to-face with others and depending on them. I believe that is completely the opposite of Bodhidharma. Practitioners today struggle, not understanding the direction of their practice after all.

So then, what was the reason for Bodhidharma's practice? It was to transmit the Buddhadharma and, in his great mercy and compassion, to save all sentient beings from delusion and suffering. Because he possessed this great mercy and compassion, he traveled for three years from India to China. What is this great mercy and compassion? Why did he desire to save all sentient beings from ignorance and suffering? Was it

158. Wearing white or various colored headbands in Japan is a way to call attention to a cause or demonstrate deep commitment to something.

because he wanted to make a name for himself or get glory or obtain some rank? Or was he perhaps ambitious and wanted to start his own business venture? Of course not. The reason why he felt compelled to spread the Buddhadharma and save all sentient beings was because all sentient beings were residing within his self. Bodhidharma's self was itself the entire limitless universe. In other words, the entire universe, this whole ten-direction world,[159] was transparent.

Therefore, precisely because his direction was to save all deluded sentient beings living in this self that is the entire universe by transmitting true zazen practice, this was his life. To be sure, Bodhidharma followed this direction and burned with devotion his entire life, but he did not depend on others to transmit the Dharma to all living things. Even if the great compassion he displayed by sincerely transmitting the Dharma to deluded beings had had no result, this effort had no small effect on the self of Bodhidharma. No matter what kind of birth Bodhidharma wanted, he was the king of the entire universe of the self, because his practice hall was itself the entire universe of the self.

Though he met the emperor, Bodhidharma understood that the true foundation of the blossoming of Buddhadharma in China had not yet been laid. Although he was undoubtedly disappointed with his meeting with the emperor, Bodhidharma was not disappointed with the self of the entire universe. One absolutely can't be disappointed with the self of the entire universe. If we look at this from the point of view of human nature, Bodhidharma made an arduous journey from India to China, a feat we can't even imagine today. However, he did not give in to feelings of despair. Looking at his travails from our own perspective we would be worried but judging by Bodhidharma's facial expression in images of him, he took all these difficulties in stride. He went to Shaolin, put

159. The "ten-direction world" includes the four cardinal directions and the four intercardinal directions of the compass, plus up and down—in other words, the entire universe.

on that mantle, and just did zazen. Dogen Zenji was inspired by this image of Bodhidharma, and wrote the following beautiful sentences in *Shobogenzo Gyoji* ("Continuous Practice"):[160]

> The First Ancestor in China came from the West as directed by his teacher, the Venerable Master Prajnatara. His three-year voyage over the raging waves of the ocean and through the seasons of frost, flowers, winds, and snows must have been more than miserable. Yet, despite these innumerable hardships, he managed to arrive in a country unknown to him. Ordinary people who hold their lives dear can't even imagine doing such a thing. This way of protecting and maintaining practice stemmed from his great compassion and his vow to transmit the Dharma and save deluded living beings. He was able to do it because he himself was the self of transmitting Dharma, and [he was living in] the world of transmitting Dharma. He could live in such a way because the entire ten-direction-world is itself the true Way; the entire ten-direction-world is nothing but his self; and that the entire ten-direction world is no other than the entire ten-direction world. Wherever you are living is a palace; there is no palace that is not an appropriate place to practice the Way. This is why [Bodhidharma] came from the West in the way he did. He had neither doubt nor fear because he was the self of saving-deluded-sentient-beings. He had neither doubt nor fear because he was living in the world of saving deluded living beings [the world of vow].

These sentences by Dogen Zenji are beautiful. He has made transparent the inexhaustible supply of Bodhidharma's lifestyle of the ten-direction world of the self. I would like to recommend that you read Dogen's words aloud over again and again.

160. Unpublished translation by Shohaku Okumura Roshi.

Bodhidharma stayed at Shaolin practicing zazen while silently facing a wall. He came all the way from India to China and, abandoned by everyone, just sat zazen. However, his zazen resonated, and someone appeared to whom he transmitted the Dharma, and eventually this person succeeded him. That was the second ancestor, Huike. However, thanks to Huike receiving the Dharma from Bodhidharma, his zazen practice also resonated, but he had to spend the rest of his days sitting zazen in anonymity. However, because his zazen also had resonance, a successor appeared. That was the Third Ancestor, Sengcan. In the same way came the Fourth Ancestor, Daoxin; the Fifth Ancestor, Hongren; and the Sixth Ancestor, Huineng. The Dharma was transmitted from each master to the next, and by a thin thread they somehow managed to get to the Sixth Ancestor. However, two other monks, Qingyuan Xingsi and Nanyue Huairang, along with many others gathered before Huineng like a cluster of heroes and spread Bodhidharma's zazen in China and further to Korea and Japan. These days, if we speak about Eastern culture, there is nothing that has not been influenced by Zen; the influence that spread from this root is huge.

Having said this, when Bodhidharma sat facing the wall for nine years at Shaolin, what would have happened if his only disciple, Huike, hadn't succeeded him? Well, without a doubt, the thin thread that connected the founder Bodhidharma to the Sixth Ancestor would have been cut and today there would be no culture of Zen and we wouldn't know anything about Bodhidharma. All traces of the man who took the trouble to travel from India to China and sat facing the wall for nine years would be gone. Also, the Second, Third, Fourth, and so on ancestors would be unknown to us, and their existences would be buried in obscurity. If we think about this, I can't help feeling that but for a coincidence of history, this could have happened.

And so, since Bodhidharma through this succession of six ancestors was able to open five petals from one flower—that is, the five schools of Zen in China—his life was adorned with this achievement. Therefore, do you think that he was first able to obtain his life because of this coincidence of history? Absolutely not! It is clear that Bodhidharma did not rely on this historical coincidence to sit facing the wall for nine years. Rather, he sat for nine years in order to practice the self that is the self of the entire universe. By focusing his life on transmitting the Dharma and saving deluded sentient beings, he was able to completely conclude his life's work. Can we say that his work of transmitting the Dharma and saving deluded sentient beings would bear fruit at some point? About this, Bodhidharma himself was unwavering and had neither the slightest doubt nor fear. What does it mean that Bodhidharma had neither doubts nor fears? It means that he assumed the self that is the self of the entire universe and just plunked himself down and sat zazen, living his life boldly and with vitality.

When we compare the life of Bodhidharma to the so-called great heroes of the world, Alexander the Great, Caesar, Napoleon, Toyotomi Hideyoshi, Tokogawa Ieyasu,[161] or more recently the villains, Hitler, Mussolini, Stalin, or Tojo, we are compelled to remember the kind of lives they lived. Those people who are called heroes or villains, as we understand when we read their biographies, all lacked direction, and they pushed away and crushed opponents. In their terrible haste to crush their opponents, they overlooked their humanity. However, once they stumbled, they were unable to take stock of themselves and their actions and, in the end, they were weak and helpless people. It seems strange to me that these people were able to stir up so much trouble. We can see the suffering that resulted from their chance appearance in the world. At the same time, we can't ignore the foolishly vain and mistaken belief of these so-called heroes and villains that it was their own power and ability, instead of historical coincidence, that caused their rise to power.

However, Bodhidharma, while also living within the coincidences

161. Warlord Toyotomi Hideyoshi (1537–1598) and Shogun Tokogawa Ieyasu (1543–1616).

of history, entrusted himself to the power of the life of the self. Surely the direction that he took for his life was to transmit the Dharma to all sentient beings and save them from suffering and delusion. However, his effectiveness was entirely due to circumstances and coincidences beyond his control. But these coincidences for certain had nothing to do with his relying on others. Rather, for Bodhidharma all living beings were nothing other than inhabitants of the entire ten-direction universe, and the direction he chose for his life was to transmit the Buddhadharma, practicing as the self of the ten-direction universe to save all sentient beings from delusion and suffering. Bodhidharma survived living the life of the straightforward self of the entire universe. What a powerful and reliable sitting practice! What a daring and fearless way of life, this life treading on this great earth!

We can compare Bodhidharma's way of life not only to the so-called heroes and villains of history but also to typical Buddhist priests these days. Many priests are busy pushing others aside and taking down others right before our eyes. They strive for fame, position, and money. They lack direction in their life, and in the end they stir up confusion in the world. Stumbling, beaten up by others, when they must return to their own self, they expose their small selves, hopeless and weak.

In the latter question section of the Kannon-gyo, Inexhaustible Mind Bodhisattva asks, "World Honored One, why does Perceiver of the Cries of the World Bodhisattva travel around this world? How does he teach the Dharma for the sake of all sentient beings? What sort of power of skillful means does he have?" The phrase, "this person who travels around the world," can also be applied to Bodhidharma, although his travels were quieter. Because we can't find other examples like this, that is why I speak about Bodhidharma here. But I'm not speaking about his way of life simply to tell his story. Right now, here in the twentieth century, the person I revere most is Bodhidharma. His example gives me the power to live truthfully. I feel joy because he shows me a true direction in life. Truly, Buddhadharma must be based on the study of one's true self.

20. Everything We Encounter Is Our Life

Traveling in the Bodhisattva's World

I was once told by my teacher Sawaki Roshi,

> Religious practice is like going on a Dutch date: each person pays their own way. Likewise, each person does their own practice, working hard at kneading, softening, and dissipating their self-centered ways. Don't hate this or like it. Just disentangle the love and hate in yourself, letting it break up and scatter. Someone who acquires this skill is said to be a well-trained practitioner.

Most people don't feel the need to engage in religious practice. Though most people rarely come to this realization, if they do, they don't know how to begin and so they ask, "How should I practice?" The direction of practice becomes a problem. At that point they start to read religious texts and listen to talks and do all kinds of useless activities that don't point out the correct way to train. My teacher's plain and simple words—"disentangle the love and hate of our self-centered egos, break it up and scatter it"—are a straightforward expression that is rarely encountered. Let's follow his bold teaching and diligently make efforts to study and practice day and night. After hearing these words by Sawaki Roshi, even someone as minor as me feels like I have some headphones on, and his words are ringing in my ears.

For example, when I have feelings of desire or anger, I try to disentangle these feelings. Or, when I'm in the depths of despair or some sort of difficulty or feeling dissatisfied, I disentangle myself. I disentangle myself by chanting wholeheartedly, "I take refuge in the sound that sees the world." Or "I take refuge in the undefiled universe." Or "I take refuge in Kanzeon." Incidentally, when you feel you want to shout out sounds of attachment to the world or hatred of the world, but instead chant the undefiled sound, "I take refuge in Kanzeon," and unravel these feelings, at that time the Bodhisattva Kanzeon is realized.

In other words, through the sound of the undefiled chanting of *Namu Kanzeon*, when we soften the craving to satisfy our selfish desires and disentangle from them, a boundless and infinite attitude is realized. No matter what happens, no matter what thing, no matter what person, everything is a manifestation of the big mind, everything we encounter is our life. In the case of Bodhidharma, this boundless attitude of big mind is revealed in his story as the self of the ten-direction world. Speaking of this self, when we get full of ourselves because we think it is easy to realize enlightenment through a single effort, and in one gulp encounter the circumstances in which we swallow the entire universe—in other words, have some fake enlightenment experience—that is not correct practice. True practice is about kneading, massaging, and dissipating the ego or karmic self and accepting the resulting fresh, new self, as all that I encounter is my life.

Dogen wrote in *Shobogenzo Genjokoan* ("Actualizing the Fundamental Point"),

> Therefore, if there are fish that would swim or birds that would fly only after investigating the entire ocean or sky, they would find neither path nor place. When we make this very place our own, our practice becomes the actualization of reality. When we make this path our own, our activity naturally becomes actualized reality. . . . In the same way, when a person engages in practice-enlightenment in the Buddha Way, as the person realizes one dharma, the person

permeates that dharma; as the person encounters one practice, the person [fully] practices that practice.

I am not saying that the self of the ten-direction world is the same size as the ten-direction world. Whatever happens, whatever object, whatever person, it is precisely the practice of breaking up our egos and practicing magnanimous mind—accepting that whatever I encounter is my life—this practice is called the self of the ten-direction world, the self of the whole universe.

The person who practices by means of magnanimous mind is called a bodhisattva. *Bodhisattva* refers to those who find magnanimous mind within the ultimate reality of the self—that is, supreme wisdom. According to the *Dazhidu lun* (Treatise on the Great Prajnaparamita):

> In Chinese, *bodhi* (awakening) is called unsurpassable wisdom. *Sattva* means a "living being," or this also refers to magnanimous mind. Those who arouse magnanimous mind, for the sake of attaining unsurpassed wisdom, are called bodhisattvas. They wish to allow all living beings to practice the unsurpassable Way. This person is called a bodhisattva.[162]

Furthermore, Kanzeon Bosatsu is also referred to as the bodhisattva of great compassion, or the bodhisattva of mercy; this is the mind that comes about when the ego is softened by practice and dissipated (a state of ultimate emptiness) and when the magnanimous mind comes alive as "Everything I encounter is my life." To the degree that this magnanimous

162. *Dazhidu lun* (Treatise on the Great Prajnaparamita), *Taisho Tripitaka* 1509, 25:380. The *Dazhidu lun* is an extensive commentary on the Sutra of Transcendental Wisdom in Twenty-Five Thousand Lines. This sutra was translated from Sanskrit to Chinese by the famous translator Kumarajiva (312–413). The original Sanskrit version is lost, but the Chinese translation survives though Kumarajiva. The sutra and its commentary influenced all the major schools of Chinese Buddhism.

mind is enabled, for all sentient beings the mind of unparalleled love is born.

Also, from the *Dazhidu lun*: "Objectless Compassion (not dependent on who the person you are trying to help is) is born from ultimate emptiness."[163] And from the Perfection of Wisdom Sutra: "Because they have nothing to gain, bodhisattvas should not depart from this thought of great compassion."[164]

At this point, when we are chanting *Namu Kanzeon*, we are rescued from our suffering by this hand of the great compassion of the Bodhisattva Kanzeon. However, while chanting, we ourselves become none other than Kanzeon Bosatsu and we awaken the objectless great compassion and extend it to all living beings. This is because wholeheartedly chanting the name softens and dissipates our self-centered egos, and the activity of the magnanimous mind is always none other than the activity of the mind of great compassion.

I understand that our efforts are feeble and might seem small. However, even if they are weak, if they produce the magnanimous mind, this is already the Bodhisattva Kanzeon. We humans are not perfect beings, but I think that aiming for this is something that we should get comfortable with. It is said in the *Dazhidu lun*, "We are bodhisattvas," and I think these words are a strong affirmation of our reason for living. We just continue to suffer through this samsara world, but living doesn't mean just making a living for ourselves or nourishing our bodies; rather, it is cultivating magnanimous mind so that everything we meet becomes our life and we can relax in the world of no-gain, the spacious world of the bodhisattva.

The Diamond Sutra says, "I should give up all my possessions. I should join my mind together with all living beings." These words clearly reveal the bodhisattva ideal. I often reflect upon these words, because they

163. *Taisho Tripitaka* 1509, 25:442.
164. *Taisho Tripitaka* 1509, 8:272.

clearly describe the human image of the ideal of Mahayana Buddhism. Indeed, I also believe that it gives a real-life goal for us living in today's society, and it paints a portrait of the ideal direction for future members of human society.

Broadly speaking, in Western history up until now, there have been two completely different cultural currents of thought. The first arose in ancient Greece, then declined in the Middle Ages and has recently become dominant again. It is the humanistic view that glorifies human action. The other current of thought, which was rooted in Christianity and dominated the Middle Ages, focused on heaven and the afterlife. This is a broad generalization, but we can still detect the influence of these two points of view even today.

For example, in the realm of art we can see these two separate currents reflected in the symbolism of the human form. In the art of ancient Greece, there is a preference for sculpting the beautiful naked form, such as that of Venus, which glorifies the physical human body. But when we reach the Christian era in the Middle Ages, we see the beautiful Madonna concealed under thick clothing, and believers were admonished to seek the beauty of truth only in the heavens. Following the Renaissance, the thick clothing was stripped off again and the nude form was again a preferred theme in painting and sculpture. After that, the cultural current of seeking beauty in the human body has continued to this day.

These days, however, the glorification of human beings is coming to an end, and we no longer define beauty in terms of nude figures. Instead, it seems we are on a new degenerate path that glorifies pornographic images of animalistic acts.

In contrast, in the *Dazhidu lun*, it is said that, as a bodhisattva, I should give up all worldly possessions. Christianity also teaches that we must disavow the earthly world. The sutra admonishes us, "I should join my mind together with all living beings." Isn't this precisely the reason for living the bodhisattva way? It is a new rational ideal of a third way for humans to live, beyond the two extremes of humanism and religiosity. I believe that presenting the bodhisattva as a human ideal, so that shouldering a role in world history must come to be thought of as an important thing.

This Mahayana ideal of the bodhisattva came into ascendancy during a period of world history known as the Axial Age, from the eighth to the third century BCE, when the region of northwest India was engaged in active trade and lively cultural exchange with Greece. The cultures of India and Greece interacted with each other in a balanced collaboration. In *Civilizing India: A Historical Overview*,[165] the eminent French scholar Sylvain Levi, who specialized in Sanskrit and Indian history, wrote that ancient India was mostly able to resist cultural assimilation by the Greeks. But if there was an attempt to join Western Greek culture with Eastern Indian culture, it would have happened in the third or second century BCE. It was during this pivotal era that the bodhisattva ideal of humanity was born.

The emergence of the bodhisattva ideal on the world stage was a significant moment, but regrettably cultural exchange between East and West faded. Eastern culture stagnated, and two thousand years have passed without the ideal of the bodhisattva playing an active role on the world stage. But now we are again in an era of a blending of Western and Eastern cultures, so this is a perfect time for the bodhisattva ideal to be enthusiastically embraced. As we bring about this age of the ascendency of the bodhisattva, we must remember these simple words from the *Dazhidu lun*: "We are bodhisattvas." I would like to ask from the bottom of my heart that we create a new era based on the bodhisattva ideal of humanity. But it is not just a matter of specifying to people a true-life stance or making others aware of their role in world history. If you are practicing in an attempt to gain freedom from birth, old age, sickness, suffering, and death for yourself only, then you are not fostering Buddhism anew.

165. The original French title is *L'Inde civilisatrice: aperçu historique* (1938).

What do you think about the fact that these days people just want to be entertained, and some people seek pleasure through gambling and sightseeing? As for me, these days I just do zazen, far away from that raging stream. I've never played pachinko even once. I think television is foolish, and I don't even listen to the radio. But people out in the world like to play, and it seems to me that, more than ever, all they do is run around wildly looking for excitement. People seem to think that this play is really living, and they call it true culture. My response to this type of frenetic world is, "People these days have run out of reasons to live." If people have truly discovered their reason for living, then why are they obsessed with constantly seeking entertainment and pleasure?

When people encounter the reality of their lives, they see no other way than to become absorbed in so-called fun. Their mind is separated from the life of the self. Seeing that people all over the world rush around wildly in pursuit of entertainment, pleasure, gambling, and sightseeing, we can realize that people lack direction in their lives and feel no passion for living. I would like to recommend that we play in the playground of the Bodhisattva Kanzeon.

The play of Kanzeon is not the kind of play that separates your mind from your own life. We don't need to engage in the kind of play that paralyzes us. Rather, we should have the attitude that "everything I encounter is my life." We are living the self of the entire ten-direction world, so no matter which way we turn it is the play of discovering the true purpose of our life. These days if play separates us from our lives and if we just end up playing out our lives, then the play of the bodhisattva is playing in our lives; let's play the play of our lives. I think that we need to take care of our lives and think more seriously about our purpose in living.

What really is this traveling in our lives? In a single phrase, it is as Sawaki Roshi said, kneading and softening our self-centered egos and dissipating this mind: "Everything I encounter is my life." It gives importance to practicing here and now with no exception, but there are all sorts of encounters in our lives.

Let's consider the second question posed to the Buddha by Inexhaustible Mind Bodhisattva: "World Honored One, why does Perceiver of the Cries of the World Bodhisattva travel around in this world?" This travel is like Bodhidharma's travels mentioned earlier—truly a unique and wonderful type of travel. However, unfortunately it is difficult for us to comprehend the deeper meaning of Bodhidharma's story, so I would like to attempt to relate this form of travel to our daily lives through an appreciation of the Kannon-gyo—that is, the Avalokiteshvara Sutra.

21. The Thirty-Three Forms of Avalokiteshvara

In Japan, the Kannon-gyo is frequently chanted, so even people who are not particularly familiar with Buddhism have probably heard the sutra chanted out loud. The words relating to the section on the teaching on the thirty-three forms of Kannon are chanted again and again. Inexhaustible Mind Bodhisattva asks the Buddha, "World-Honored One, why does Perceiver of the Cries of the World Bodhisattva travel around in this world? How does he teach the Dharma for the sake of the living? What sort of power of skillful means does he have?" In reply, the Buddha gives a list of the thirty-three forms of Kannon. The Buddha says, "Good son, if living beings in any land need someone in the body of a buddha in order to be saved, Perceiver of the Cries of the World Bodhisattva appears as a buddha and teaches the Dharma to them." And the Buddha then proceeds to list thirty-two more forms in which the bodhisattva can appear to people in need.

At the time that these sutras were created, Indian society must have moved at a very relaxed pace. The sutra repeats the questions and answers again and again, and it is hard for us nowadays to stay focused. But if you think about it, a sutra is a book about religion; it's not a book that you read for entertainment. Reading a sutra with its monotonous repetition is relaxing and is almost like a religious practice itself. In the Kannon-gyo, the phrase "Keep in mind Kannon's powers" is repeated again and again, solemnly reverberating and invoking the power of Kannon when we encounter various difficulties. The repetition of this rhythmical meter gives the reader a feeling of peace.

In this short book, I can offer only a broad perspective, so I will omit a detailed explanation of each of the many forms of Avalokiteshvara. However, among those forms are the eight guardians of Buddhism: *devas* (gods), *nagas* (dragons and serpents), *yakshas* (nature spirits), *gandharvas* (gods of music, medicine and children), *asuras* (demigods), *garudas* (mythical bird-man creatures), *kimnaras* (another type of birdlike creature), and *mahoragas* (serpentine musicians). Of course, these are creatures of the imagination. There's a sculpture of one of these guardian-deity forms of Kannon, which looks like a crow with a long beak, and it is playing a flute and dancing. If you would like to see these images, I invite you to visit Sanjusangendo Temple in Kyoto, where wooden statues of these forms are on display.

Instead of going through the thirty-three forms one by one, we should appreciate them as various subtle states of mind that we experience from time to time. When we experience each of these states, we should not dwell upon that strange world of mythical creatures—but it is entirely appropriate to conceive of our emotional states as complex, strange, and mysterious animals. The Kannon-gyo repeatedly states that seeing each of these thirty-three forms in situations we encounter is not a matter of simply our own personal judgment.

My way of interpreting these thirty-three forms of Kannon is to see them as each fitting a particular state of mind or circumstance. Surely, all these forms have the purpose of revealing the Dharma teachings. For example, if someone is poor, sick, or in hopeless despair, Kannon transforms into the appropriate form for teaching the Dharma to them. Of course, Kannon is not limited to these thirty-three forms but in fact has unlimited forms and can transform into whatever form is best to teach the Dharma. By extension, whatever circumstances we encounter, at that time we should listen to the Dharma teachings of Kannon. This is what the Kannon-gyo is teaching.

Having said that, what we need to appreciate most in the Kannon-gyo is that when Kanzeon appears in the appropriate form to teach the

Dharma to a poor person or to someone who is ill, the sutra is not saying that Kannon preaches the Dharma so that the poor person will get rich or the sick person will recover. The word Dharma in the phrase "to teach the Dharma" refers to the Buddhadharma, the one mind, which we cannot attach a price to, the true form of the self, undefiled no matter which way we turn.

Further, in contrast to the Kannon-gyo, the false and distorted writings of the new religions in Japan all promote the idea that illnesses can be cured and that we can obtain some benefit or profit from believing in these religions. So, people listen to a talk by one of these charlatans and think that it would be wonderful if their illnesses could be cured. We are told that sickness and poverty are bad, and we must detest them. However, if we understand that sickness and poverty are part of life, then even if our disease is cured or our poverty is eased, that good fortune is only half of what life is about. That half of life when we have riches and good health will in the end be taken from us and we will face the undeniable reality that we must die naked and alone, becoming nothing. But this is not the Dharma teaching of Kanzeon. Life is a manifestation of total function; death is a manifestation of total function. For those who need someone in the body of a dying person in order to be saved, the bodhisattva appears as a dying person; for those who need someone in the body of a person taking their last gasps to be saved, Kannon appears as a person taking their last gasps. Whether we encounter life or death, no matter which way we look, this cannot be separated from Dharma teachings. The value of the truth of the Buddhadharma is hearing the Dharma teachings and wholeheartedly practicing them with your own body.

When I was little, living near me were two brothers, I-chan and Tsune-chan. I-chan was more my brother's best buddy, and since Tsune-chan and I were in the same class at grammar school and lived close to each other, we often played at each other's houses. I heard that their father worked as a railway porter carrying luggage, but he wasn't physically very strong. In those days they were poor, since he often had to take time off from work due to physical problems. The father came from Toyama Prefecture and, like many of the people in that area, he and his family were devoted Pure Land believers. The mother was especially devoted. She was also completely illiterate and couldn't read any texts, so she often went to the local Pure Land temple to listen to sermons. Later, when I was in middle school, she would often take I-chan and me along with her to the village temple to listen to sermons.

In any case, when I was in second or third grade, one day I-chan came to play with my brother, and I joined them to play on the second floor of our house. (What I'm about to relate is rather an embarrassment to my family.) My mother's aunt had come to live at our house. She didn't like that her husband had taken a mistress and brought this woman to live in their home, and that was the reason that she had come to live at our house, which was also her childhood home. My mother's aunt was ill-tempered, abrasive, and unkind. On this occasion, she became aware that I-chan was playing at our house, and she shouted from downstairs, "Hey, Yo-chan!" That was my older brother's name. "Don't play with poor children!" Both my brother and I-chan were shocked by her words, and both had sad faces. Looking as though he were about to cry, the sensitive I-chan stood up and said, "I'm leaving." My brother also stood up, not knowing what to say. I went outside with them. I don't remember what we talked about as we walked along. In any case, we eventually arrived at I-chan's house.

I-chan's mother was busy sewing. It seems that she took in needlework to supplement the family income. Their house was very small, and the three of us had to play in a narrow space alongside I-chan's mother, and naturally the conversation turned to a discussion of my aunt's behavior. I-chan said to his mother, " Mom, when we were playing at Yo-chan's house, his aunt shouted to him that he wasn't to play with poor kids. I was startled and shocked." Both my brother and I felt terrible and didn't know what to say or do. My brother and I intuitively grasped the situation, as children can. But I-chan's mom just continued to sew. When I perceived her facial profile in the soft light of the room, I saw that her calm countenance remained unchanged. I remember her face clearly to this day, and I was struck by how beautiful she was. She said to I-chan, gently and quietly, "Since we are poor, it naturally follows that people will say that to us." Then to all of us she said, " I know that our house is small, but go ahead and play here." She did not utter any words of lament, malice, or anger. Thinking about this today, even though I know that I-chan's mom couldn't read any sutras, I think that she must have absorbed deeply the true essence of Pure Land teachings and developed a deep faith during her visits to Pure Land temples to listen to sermons.

In some way, this experience made a deep impression on my brother and me, and sometimes we still talk about it. We again relive the deep impact the experience had on us. Surely people like I-chan's mother heard the phrase from the Kannon-gyo Dharma teachings, "for those who need someone in the form of a poor person in order to be freed from suffering, Kannon appears in the form of a poor person and teaches the Dharma to them." Perhaps they felt themselves to be transformed into a form of Kannon, compelled to teach the Dharma for the sake of all living beings in this corrupt world feel. Even to this day I continue to vividly recall this Dharma teaching.

Please permit me to tell you about another experience with I-chan's mother that made a deep impression on my brother and me. After the above experience, I-chan's father became increasingly weak, and he could no longer endure hard physical work. Eventually, he was diagnosed with neuralgia and was unable to work. As a result, I-chan had to drop out of middle school and go to work. However, since he was a meek child who lacked self-confidence, he didn't have what it took to thrive out in the world, and he was harassed and treated unkindly by his fellow workers.

On the other hand, his younger brother, Tsune-chan, was resourceful and capable in the commercial world, and since he was proficient at calculating with an abacus, he was able to get a job with the Bank of Japan.

It was at that time that my brother went to pay a visit to I-chan, and when he returned, he spoke with my mother and me. "I-chan's mother is truly remarkable! When I was there, I-chan said to me, 'Tsune-chan is resourceful, and I think that he will continue to be successful out in the world, but since I'm not good at my job, I don't know if I can put food on the table for Mom and Dad.' I was surprised when his mother heard him and said, 'It's wonderful that Tsune-chan will be a success. After I get old, since I will be relying on you, I-chan, my oldest son, I will entrust myself to your care. If you don't have work and become a beggar, that's OK—we'll just be beggars together.' I-chan and I both cried." My mother and I also shed tears when we heard my brother's story. These words came from I-chan's mother, who could not read a single letter. We should not lose sight of the main thread of this story; we cannot disregard the noble resolve that she was gladly willing to live in poverty as a beggar. Isn't it within this resolve that can be found the final resting place for humanity?

After that, there was a huge earthquake, and then the war, so my brother lost contact with I-chan. As of today, I haven't had any news of I-chan and his mother for over ten years, but I know that somewhere in this world she has grown old, and even if she is living as a beggar, I am sure that this woman appears to others as Kannon in the form of a beggar—if that is what is required to teach the Dharma for them. She and beings like her know no misery and travel around this world composed and blessed with an expansive view of the world.

In contrast, there are many people in the world who have a more typical point of view and say, "To be poor is misery" and "If you don't have money, you're nothing." But I would like everyone to know that there is more in this world than money. Even the sons and daughters of rich households engage in disreputable behavior, causing all types of problems. Older people sigh and say, "Living is hell," and are examples of falling into that way of thinking.

The light of religion surely speaks to this. It's not that when you cease to be poor that the light of religion shines through at last, but just being poor, or just being ill, at that point just being present in that space where you simply practice the self that we are unable to attach a price to—at that point the light of religion shines through.

In the same way, there must be a way for an older person to age gracefully, bathed in a bright and glorious light, or there must be a way for someone who is paralyzed to also live bathed in the same light. Being poor or making bad choices are phenomena of our society; sickness and old age are biological phenomena. I think that in opposition to these phenomena is the world of true religion. We can either continue to submit to societal norms, or find a way to light our lives with religion. As it says in the Amida Sutra, "The red [lotuses] radiate red light. The blue [lotuses] radiate blue light. This is called paradise [the Pure Land]." The world of true religion is what this sutra is referring to: things just as they are. The Dharma teachings in the Kannon-gyo are surely referring to the manifestation of the light of true religion.

22. Where I Place My Weak Mind

It was September 1, 1923. On that day, the father, Kanshiro, ate lunch early and left for his job at a store in Asakusa. At that time, the Kosugi family lived in the Honjoku Midori Machi area of Tokyo, and Kanshiro worked at a kimono fabric shop. The father had left for work, and the mother, Yoshi, was cleaning up, while the four-year-old girl Toyoko was putting her six-month-old sister Yasuko into a baby hammock. Suddenly everything began to shake and rock. It sounded like the great earth was groaning. It was a huge earthquake. The mother flew to the hammock and hugged the infant close to her and together with Toyoko crouched next to a large chest of drawers. The house shook and swayed, creaking terribly, and in an instant the mother and children were thrown into the depths of fear, terror, and panic.

When the initial tremors temporarily subsided, they heard the wooden clogs of someone racing around outside. The young man from the rice shop next door came flying in, yelling out, "Mrs. Kosugi, fire! Run away right now!" In a panic, she didn't know exactly what to do next, but she quickly grabbed the images of the Shinto god and the Buddha from the second floor. Cradling them in her arms, she put them together with the documents for their business and other important papers and stuffed it all together into two bundles.

The electricity, gas, and water abruptly stopped, and smoke from fires rose up. There was no time to warn the neighbors. She heard someone saying, "Go to the Honjo Clothing Depot,[166] go to the Honjo Clothing

166. The Honjo Clothing Depot (also called Hifukusho) was a large production and storage facility operated by the clothing department of the imperial Japanese army. More than 35,000 people burned to death there as a result of a whirlwind firestorm that enveloped that area on the night of September 1, 1923.

Depot," so she strapped the baby onto her back, held on to the bundles, tightly grabbed Toyoko's sleeve and hurried out of the house to the nearby Honjo Clothing Depot. On the way, she joined many others, all with panicked expressions, carrying their belongings and hurrying toward the depot. However, when she arrived, the wide-open spaces around the depot were jammed full of people and their belongings, and she saw that it was impossible to get in after all.

Masses of people were crowded around when someone said, "Let's go to Ueno," and some people started walking toward Umayabashi Bridge. Yoshi made an instant decision that Ueno was the only place to go, so with her children in tow she headed toward the bridge. When they arrived, the bridge was jammed with panicked people pushing and shoving, but she had no choice and frantically proceeded to cross, jostled by all the passersby. About halfway across, Toyoko tripped and fell. Yoshi put down her bundle and tried to pick up her daughter, but a stampede of people knocked into her before she could pick her up. At the same time, people were smashing into the baby strapped onto her back, and Yoshi struggled to shield Toyoko from being crushed. She could do little for the infant on her back, but she thought that at least she would protect Toyoko. So, she bent down over Toyoko, protecting her. As she often did in times of trouble, Yoshi began to recite the Ten-Line Kannon Sutra, *Kanzeon Namu Butsu*. As desperate people stumbled over her, she continued,

Kanzeon, I take refuge in the Buddha
We have affinity with Buddha . . .

After a while, she felt a sudden radiant aura of light and raised her head. There was no longer anyone around her, and the bridge was on fire. On either side of the bridge, both banks of the river were burning in a sea of fire, and suddenly both ends of the bridge were aflame. In an instant, the mother pulled herself together, stood Toyoko up, and they rushed across the bridge past the flames to the other side. As soon as they got across, the entire bridge collapsed.

On the other side of the bridge in Asakusa, there was a confused mass of people and fire, and Yoshi fell in with the crowd walking toward Ueno Park. When they finally arrived at the park, they started to climb the hill with the bronze statue of Takamori Saigo, and they followed the wide road into the park. Vast numbers of people were camped there under the cherry trees that line both sides of the road. Yoshi found a small space under the trees and finally was able to put down her bundles. When she took the infant off her back, she was overjoyed to find that her baby was still alive. When she checked her children's bodies, she saw that neither Toyoko nor Yasuko had any injury, and without thinking Yoshi bowed down and offered thanks to Kannon.

That night, looking down from Ueno hill, only the direction of Sakuramachi was not burning; the three other directions were seas of fire. All through the night, people walked up and down on the park's central road, carrying wooden tags and lanterns suspended from poles, calling out the names of their loved ones. Yoshi was unable to find her husband, but she and Toyoko continued to call out into the dark with all their might, listening for a response. But there was no response, not that night nor for the next two days.

The father, Kanshiro, had felt the huge earthquake as he was walking to the store, and he immediately turned around and hurried back toward his home. But as he was walking, he encountered a wall of fire, so he decided to head for Ueno, narrowly escaping with his life. After that, every day he tried to get through the fire-devastated area to return to his home in Honjo, but there were no posted notices from his family. However, as he passed the Honjo Clothing Depot, he saw piles of burned corpses, and in the Sumida River countless drowned bodies were floating up and down the river with the tides, so he was forced to assume that his wife and daughters were all dead. Finally, on the fifth day after the quake, despondent, he visited the Asakusa Kannon Temple. After walking around aimlessly, he resolved to die, and he stopped drinking and eating.

Until that day, the rest of the Kosugi family had been going to Ueno hill to get emergency food distributions, but on that day, Yoshi decided to go to the Asakusa Kannon Temple to pray. Suddenly Yoshi and Toyoko saw Kanshiro. Without thinking, they yelled out, "Hey, Dad, you're back!"—which is equivalent to exclaiming with great joy, "Thank goodness you survived!" And that is how the family was reunited.

Toyoko, who told me this story, is now a Buddhist nun, my older-sister nun ordained before me, with the Buddhist name Yuho Kuga.[167] I heard this story about the Tokyo earthquake and fire directly from her. When I was twelve years old, I had experienced the same event. On the first of September, our home, which was in the Hongo Moto-machi district of Tokyo, burned down, and my family and I also spent the night in Ueno Park. Her story is very real to me, so I wrote it down exactly as she told it to me.

All the members of the Kosugi family are quite remarkable. I'm going to abbreviate the particulars of their family circumstances, but in any case, the entire family—including the father, Kanshiro; the mother, Yoshi; the elder daughter, Toyoko, also known as Kuge-san; and the younger daughter, Yasuko, who was a baby at the time; as well as a brother born afterward named Daiyu—all five family members were ordained as Buddhist clerics. These days it's not unusual for a temple priest to have his wife and children receive ordination and live in a temple building, operating as a close-knit family unit. But in the case of the Kosugis, each family member went their separate way, each leaping into serious Buddhist practice. This example is rare, in fact almost unheard of. In any case, the entire family, from the days when the father and mother were lay practitioners, was certainly a remarkable family of faithful believers.

167. When Toyoko Kosugi became ordained, she was probably adopted into the family of the head priest of the temple where she resided and took that family name of Kuga. This is a common practice in Japan. For our purposes, the Kosugi family and the Kuga family are one and the same.

When I originally heard the story about the dangerous situation on the Umayabashi Bridge—when the child fell, and her mother protected her while desperately chanting the Ten-Line Kannon-gyo, and then somehow got the children across the bridge just as it was about to collapse—I discounted it as one of those so-called miraculous religious tales about Kannon that you hear. However, over time, I gradually changed my mind and started to think of it as not just some miracle tale. Surely, after you've been saved from such a desperate situation, you can think of yourself as having gained some benefit from chanting Kannon's name. But the reason why the mother, Yoshi, continued to chant the Ten-Line Kannon-gyo was because her situation was hopeless, and she had no other recourse except to chant. This is often called "calling on a god when you are suffering"—that is, calling on a god when in distress when you think that you are trapped and there is no possible way out. I think that it is the equivalent of a child calling out for its mother in a panic. I call it a word of exclamation, and calling out or chanting the name of Kanzeon Bodhisattva wholeheartedly is surely an exclamation, a primal voice that emanates from within you when not thinking of yourself.

I would now like to give you some background about the Lotus Sutra as a foundation of Mahayana Buddhism.

The Lotus Sutra sets the context for the Kannon-gyo. The Buddhist religion is in turn the background for the Lotus Sutra, and our lives must be the foundation for the Buddhist religion. Conversely, we must view this religion called Buddhism from the standpoint of our lives, and moreover we must see the Kannon-gyo from the foundation of the Lotus Sutra.

Up to this point, I haven't discussed the place of the Kannon-gyo, which has as its background the Lotus Sutra. Here, at the end of this book, I would like to expand on this connection. However, explaining what kind of sutra the Lotus Sutra is is a complex undertaking. For now, I will give you the gist. For me the most important teachings of the Lotus

Sutra are as follows:

1. Everywhere in the ten directions is within Buddha land. (Similarly, in the opening statement of Dogen's *Shobogenzo Hokke Ten Hokke* ("The Flower of Dharma Turns the Flower of Dharma") is the phrase "The Buddha lands of the ten directions are just dharma blossoms.")[168]
2. All beings are true reality.
3. The eternal truth is truly actualized.

These three expressions represent the primary teachings of the Lotus Sutra.

However, if we are suddenly told, "Everywhere in the ten directions is within Buddha land" and "All beings are true reality" and "The eternal truth is truly actualized," then we think that these statements must be talking about something outside of ourselves, since they are totally outside of our daily reality. That is because we feel that we are confined to our ephemeral world.

But the world of the Lotus Sutra is not the world we see with our eyes. The sutra is teaching us that "only among buddhas can the true character of all things be fathomed."[169]

What we see with our eyes is different from what the Buddha sees. Naturally, our yardstick is totally different from the Buddha's. Chickens can't see at night, just as owls can't see during the day, and naturally people can't see the Buddha lands due to the blinders of their karmic consciousness. However, if we talk about individuals, each person's point of view depends on a mishmash of genetic inheritance, circumstances, customs, education, and experiences. Their thinking develops from these influences.

168. From Kazuaki Tanahashi, ed., *Treasury of the True Dharma Eye* (Boston: Shambhala Publications, 2010), 180.

169. Reeves, *Lotus Sutra*, 76.

The Buddha fathoms the true character of all things, but we are unaware of the Buddha's truth because our own awareness is based on our random points of view and our fleeting life circumstances. The Lotus Sutra comprises the teachings through the Buddha's eyes and words exactly as they are, and as such it is referred to as the king of all the Buddhist sutras. So, for us as Buddhist practitioners it is an essential teaching, not something developed from our random karmic delusions or personal points of view. Rather, it is opening the hand of thought to these delusions. We need to immediately settle down right here with "everywhere in the ten directions is within Buddha land," "all beings are true reality," and "the eternal truth is truly actualized." All of these are lines from the Lotus Sutra, and we must deepen our understanding of them.

Since we are living the truth of the reality of our life right now, how deeply can we clarify this truth? This is exactly what Shakyamuni was talking about when he said to his disciples before he died, "Respect and follow the precepts," and in Dogen's words, "Practice and enlightenment are one."

It is said that faith allows your mind to be clear and pure,[170] and truly because we are living out the reality of life of the Buddha's "everywhere in the ten directions is within Buddha land," "all beings are true reality," and "the eternal truth is truly actualized." It is precisely deepening and purifying this truth that is perceiving the precepts of Shakyamuni, and that practice and enlightenment are one.

This is the true gateway to Buddhist practice, the main thread. However, while we are alive in this body, no matter what we encounter in life, how much can we truly incorporate into our lives these three teachings found in the Lotus Sutra?

On the one hand, Buddhism is the Buddha world of the ten directions, no matter which way we turn. We don't need to become confused or make a commotion or struggle with this. On the other hand, ordinary

170. From Nagarjuna's *Treasury of Abhidharma.*

flesh-and-blood people like me are not confident that they understand key Buddhist ideas found in the Lotus Sutra, such as "everywhere in the ten directions is within Buddha land" and "all beings are true reality" and "the eternal truth is truly actualized."

In other words, speaking the unvarnished truth, the truth of ordinary people even when they try and power through—what do you do when you lose all your self-confidence? That is the exact time when *Namu Kanzeon Bosatsu* voices itself—you say it without thinking, from the depths of your despair—and the power of Kannon will work to free you from your suffering. As is said at the beginning of the Kannon-gyo, "When living beings experience suffering and without thinking wholeheartedly call the name, they will be freed, because of this he is called Kanzeon (Perceiver of the Cries of the World Bodhisattva)."

If you consider the Kannon-gyo on a surface level, it does not seem to fit in with the rest of the Lotus Sutra. In fact, it seems like a separate teaching. Indeed, scholars these days consider that the Kannon-gyo was a separate sutra added to the Lotus Sutra.[171]

As for me, I don't agree at all. The way I understand the Lotus Sutra is that it teaches three main ideas: Everywhere in the ten directions is within Buddha land. All beings are true reality. The eternal truth is truly actualized. These messages reappear in the Kannon-gyo and in my opinion complete the Lotus Sutra. The Kannon-gyo speaks to the hearts and minds of ordinary people and merges into the main thread of the Lotus Sutra.

As I described in the first chapter, ever since I worked making charcoal in the remote mountains in Shimane Prefecture in 1944, I have read the

171. This has not been verified. However, the Kannon-gyo is read and chanted by itself as if it were a separate sutra to this day. Here Uchiyama Roshi is making the point that the doctrines of the Kannon-gyo do not diverge from the main doctrines of the Lotus Sutra.

Kannon-gyo daily. In the fall of 1953, I hand-copied the Kannon-gyo in Japanese. At the end of the copy, I wrote this verse:

> Even if I am not aware of it, since all beings are experiencing suffering, I wholeheartedly chant the name.
> Even if I am not aware of it, since all beings obtain freedom, I wholeheartedly chant the name.
> Even if I am not aware of it, since Kanzeon freely travels all Buddha lands to free all sentient beings, I wholeheartedly chant the name.
> Even if I am not aware of it, since I wholeheartedly chant the name, I wholeheartedly chant the name.

In 1958 and 1959, I wrote the manuscript for this book in order to set down my thoughts about my personal, wholehearted chanting of Kanzeon's name. To summarize, I would say that, as an ordinary person, all you can do is ordinary practice. Buddhist truth is not something we can become aware of on our own. If we create yardsticks based on our own awareness, we will not understand the true meaning of suffering. We will have a mistaken view based on what ordinary people typically think of as suffering. Also, as for being emancipated from our suffering by our own innate power, even when wholeheartedly chanting the name of Kanzeon, that too is simply a misdirected action. From a Buddhist perspective, it is important not to measure things with your own personal yardstick.

As ordinary people, we always hope to satisfy our personal desires. Even if we can satisfy our wishes, are we truly content? No, the desires of ordinary people are endless. We are always dissatisfied, and we are always chasing after our unfulfilled desires. Unable to satisfy our desires, we act like grumbling, spoiled children.

Of course, as living beings our desires are important—for example, we need to feed ourselves or we will die—and it is precisely the efforts we make to fulfill these desires that rule our animal-like actions. However, we are not simply animals. We have higher-level spirits, so I hope that whatever path you take, you will discover the ultimate and immovable place to which to return and live your life there. Chanting *Namu Kanzeon Bosatsu* is the ultimate voice. It is the final resting place for our life, the ultimate cry for help when we have nowhere else to go and don't know what to do.

The cry of *Namu Kanzeon Bosatsu* is not limited to cataclysmic events like the fire on the bridge. In my own case, when I look back on my past and think about my own life, there were many times when I didn't know which path to take. I believe that many people have experienced a similar confusion. As a result, they suddenly fall into a psychological slump, get depressed, or become neurotic, even though they are grown adults. Even elderly people start grumbling. At these times, people don't know how to approach the situation. In my case, I chant *Namu Kanzeon Bosatsu*. It is my ultimate cry for help.

This ultimate cry for help is not limited to calling out *Namu Kanzeon Bosatsu*. You can call *Namu Amida Butsu*, *Namu Shakamuni Butsu* (I take refuge in Shakyamuni Buddha), or *Namu Kie Sanbo* (I take refuge in the Three Jewels: Buddha, Dharma, and Sangha). Christ called out before his crucifixion in the garden of Gethsemane: "My father, if it is possible, take this cup of suffering from me! Yet not what I want, but what you want."[172] I must say that this central theme, irrespective of denomination, is the true essence of religion.

This cry for help, *Namu Kanzeon Bosatsu*, which comes from arriving at the end with no place else to go, is a very serious thing, and we should continuously deepen this practice. But it should encompass everything we meet with in life, not just what we encounter in times of distress. We need to keep in mind, "taking refuge in the sound that perceives the world." Exactly this is the activity of the thirty-three forms of Kannon,

172. Matthew 26:39.

and I believe we must make great effort to continue to energetically engage in this practice. Holding this "taking refuge in the sound that perceives the world" in everything we encounter, we need to get past our thoughts and perceptions as ordinary people. As it says in the Sutra of Contemplation on Buddha Amitayus (also known as the Meditation Sutra),

> Although our eyes hindered by delusion do not see,
> Amitabha's great compassion always illuminates us tirelessly.[173]

> *Namu Kanzeon Bosatsu*
> In the Buddha-lands of the ten directions
> Even if we don't perceive it,
> Everyhere in the ten directions is within Buddha land.
> *Namu Kanzeon Bosatsu*.

173. From Shinran's *Shoshinge* (Verse of True Faith).

Afterword

When *Appreciating the Kannon-gyo* was first published in 1968, I included the following afterword:

> I hope that I can live a life of truth. That means that I want to live according to a religion that teaches me about the most important things in life. And so, ever since being ordained as a Buddhist monk I have practiced zazen as much as possible. At the same time, during the course of my life of Buddhist practice, I have encountered circumstances in which I couldn't practice zazen, times when I was incapacitated by illness when I chanted, "I take refuge in the sound that perceives the world" (*namu yo o kanzuru oto*). This is what I mean when I say through my life of zazen practice and my practice of calling out, or chanting, I have reflected on, thoroughly digested, and come to appreciate these practices and expanded my appreciation of the Kannon-gyo. Because of this, though this book is about my own religious life, taking into account the practice of zazen and calling out/chanting, I believe that I'm talking about the practice of the East.

From July 1958 to May 1960, *Appreciating the Kannon-gyo* appeared serially in *Evening Glow*, a magazine published by Myogenji Temple in Nagoya. I wanted to edit all of these writings into a single book but was unable to at that time. Now I feel keenly that the most important thing for me to do, in this last phase of my life, is to document my life of religious practice.

When I wrote the pieces for *Evening Glow*, I could not write everything that I wanted to say. I hoped that at some later point I would be able to say what I wanted to say, and so I wrote the original afterward.

When I finally passed seventy years old, I understood why I had been unable to express myself when I was younger. I wrote this new version with the intention of adding it to the original book. In the meantime, the first edition of the book went out of print. Finally, this year I decided to republish the book and eliminated the last chapter. Instead, I added chapter 22, "Where I Place My Weak Mind." I included this chapter because I feel that we must discuss the Kannon-gyo in connection with the foundational background of the Lotus Sutra. It's been thirty years since I first started to publish in *Evening Glow*, and twenty years since the first book was published. Last year, the book took its current form, and I am grateful that I have lived long enough to finally accomplish my original intention.

Also, the new version of the book includes chapters taken from a talk I gave at Muryoji Temple in Nagano Prefecture in the summer of last year (1985) on the Ten-Line Kannon-gyo. The Ten-Line Kannon-gyo is a sutra that I have had in my heart since my twenties, and I felt I had to include it in this book. My personal experiences are woven into this book, and I think the Ten-Line Kannon-gyo is particularly closely connected to my life. I hope that you too will form an intimate connection with it.

Kosho Uchiyama

1986

Afterword by Shusoku Kushiya[174]

For Uchiyama Roshi, realizing Kannon is just sitting zazen. When we place our left hand over our right hand and fold our legs in the half or full lotus position, just leaving everything to our posture, we realize Kannon ourselves and simultaneously become one with the great earth and sentient beings. At the same time, we may find liberation in our own life.

This book, published in July 1986 by Hakujusha Publishers, was a revised reissue of an earlier version of *Appreciating the Kannon-gyo and the Ten-Line Kannon-gyo*.

At the time that Uchiyama Roshi retired as abbot of Antaiji Temple due to a body weakened by illness, he was no longer able to endure the long hours of zazen of a sesshin. Late in life, he chanted the nenbutsu as the main thread of his religious practice. He once said, "I am no longer able to do zazen. If I keep talking about zazen as though I'm still sitting zazen, that would be a lie. So, while clearly admitting that I can't sit anymore, I am still committed to a life of religious practice. As I have said many times before, everything that I encounter in life is my life. I have made this essential attitude the living foundation of my life. One part of this essential attitude toward religious practice is sitting zazen, and another part is chanting the nenbutsu. If I didn't have this attitude, then, having become old and sick and unable to do zazen, my life of religious practice would have been finished."

174. Shusoku Kushiya was ordained by Uchiyama Roshi and practiced under him at Antaiji. After Uchiyama's retirement, Kushiya left Antaiji and moved near Uchiyama's residence and assisted him until Roshi died in 1998.

Chanting the name of Kannon in supplication, he lost his wife at a young age. He also felt compelled to invoke the name of Kannon when he was doing backbreaking work in the snowy mountains of Shimane Prefecture, collecting wood to make charcoal. Then late in his religious life he engaged in the rich practice of chanting the nenbutsu. Roshi wrote this book based on his many years of chanting, but the book also arose from his deep and earnest zazen practice.

Finding the deep meaning of Uchiyama Roshi's words is to deepen the life of the self. I think that as we discover the deeper meanings of Roshi's words, he illuminates and allows us to discover, clarify, and deepen our religious beliefs. When we experience suffering and sadness, we want to run away and we chant Kannon's name, but I don't think we are helped when we call out to Kannon at that time. However, we might say to ourselves, "I don't think this is helping," but when we chant, without knowing it or perceiving it, we are taken into the bosom of Kanzeon Bosatsu.

There are times in our lives when we can't help calling out Kannon's name. When we suffer and have nowhere else to turn, we wholeheartedly chant the name of Kanzeon Bosatsu. Then our suffering becomes transparent in our minds. At these times of suffering, we are compelled to turn to Kannon, and the bodhisattva grants us an inestimably precious gift. When we give our bodies over to the power of Kannon, and when we wholeheartedly and overflowingly chant the name of Kannon, thoughts and events become like the faint sounds of distant ocean waves, and within the energy from the voice of our sadness, sadness just becomes sadness, and it is as if we are embraced by a strong white light. At these times I think that perhaps we are embraced by the limitless compassion of Kannon.

Entering samadhi through hearing, considering, and practicing,
The upright and solemn self appears in the sacred face.

I proclaim to the pilgrims to make this meaning clear.
Guanyin [Kannon] does not abide on Potalaka Mountain.[175]

What Dogen Zenji is saying is that when he calmed his mind entering samadhi [i.e., sitting zazen and letting go of the hand of thought], the face of the self became the sacred face of Kannon. We might tend to believe that Kannon at Mount Potalaka is some kind of god with divine supernatural powers, but that is not the case. Kannon as viewed from the perspective of the Buddhadharma must be the true form of the self, which is zazen. The function of the innumerable eyes (on the thousand arms) of Kannon[176] is absolute and a normal part of everyday life. We are already living out the life of our self right here right now.

Because this is absolute, we are unable to measure our thoughts. Even so, all of us ordinary human beings always think only about our own problems. We think that we completely understand when things are good, when we are valued by others, and understand what's happening to us. When it comes to Buddhist practice, for us it's not about listening to the Buddha's teaching and practice, or faith, or enlightenment—the problem for us is to what extent we are able to take to heart these things themselves. Uchiyama Roshi's words are clear on this point:

175. There are two versions of this poem. The one used here is ascribed to Menzan Zuiho (1683–1769) and appeared in a revised edition of Dogen's biography. The other version is found in *Dōgen's Extensive Record*, 621:

[Guanyin is found] amid hearing, considering, practicing, and truly verifying the mind,
Why seek appearances of her sacred face within a cave?
I proclaim that pilgrims must themselves awaken.
Guanyin does not abide on Potalaka Mountain.

Guanyin is the Chinese name for Kannon, and Potalaka Mountain is the Japanese name for Putuoshan. Both poems are unpublished translations by Shohaku Okumura.

176. Images of Kannon often depict the bodhisattva with a thousand arms with an eye on each hand to see the sounds of the world in order to liberate all sentient beings from suffering.

> The most important thing to understand about the Buddhadharma is that we should not use our personal ideas, concepts, or perceptions to measure what we experience in our lives. We must not use these as the standard to judge things by.

This attitude came to fruition in the afterword that he composed for the book. Regarding just chanting, the phrase "without perceiving it" shows the depth of the act of chanting, and it also shows the depth of sitting zazen, giving that act a form or structure. In other words, it is the attitude of living by just sitting, letting go of the hand of thought. In opposition to this is the life of not sitting. When the wind blows it does not restrain us with its embrace, and so it is refreshing and invigorating. The wind blows due to all types of atmospheric conditions, but the wind that we feel blowing right here, right now, though it may be partially blocked by something, is just blowing. In the same way, we are living as the result of some deep and complex reasons that we can't comprehend.

I believe that Uchiyama Roshi felt that anything and everything he experienced was the divine power of Kannon. He walked continuously on that path. Throughout his life, he experienced everything he met in life as just his life. He bowed to the vast sky, to the roadside flowers, to anyone and everyone, to joy and sadness, and to all of Kannon's blessings. He chanted, felt calm, and walked the endless path (of practice) subsumed in the life of the universe: all that exists is the voice chanting *Namu Kanzeon Bosatsu*. Everywhere is the light of *Namu Kanzeon*.

Here is Uchiyama Roshi's last poem that he completed on the day he died:

With Deep Reverence

Joining the right hand with the left—bowing with deep reverence
Wholeheartedly striving to become one with God and
  Buddha—bowing with deep reverence
Wholeheartedly striving to become one with Everything
  I meet—bowing with deep reverence
Wholeheartedly striving to become one with all myriad things—
  bowing with deep reverence
Wholeheartedly striving to join Life with Life—bowing with
  deep reverence

—Shusoku Kushiya

Appendix 1
The Kannon-gyo, Chapter 25 of the Lotus Sutra

The Universal Gateway of the Bodhisattva Regarder of the Cries of the World

At that time the Bodhisattva Inexhaustible Mind got up from his seat, bared his right shoulder, put his palms together facing the Buddha, and said, "World-Honored One, for what reason does the Bodhisattva Regarder of the Cries of the World have the name Regarder of the Cries of the World?"

The Buddha answered Inexhaustible Mind Bodhisattva: "Good son! If there were countless hundreds of thousands of billions of living beings experiencing suffering and agony who heard of this Regarder of the Cries of the World Bodhisattva, and wholeheartedly called his name, Regarder of the Cries of the World Bodhisattva would immediately hear their cries, and all of them would be freed.

"If anyone who embraces the name of Regarder of the Cries of the World Bodhisattva falls into a great fire, the fire will not burn that person, due to the divine authority and power of that bodhisattva. If anyone, carried away by a flood, calls his name, that person will immediately reach some shallows. If there are hundreds of thousands of billions of beings who, in search of gold, silver, lapis lazuli, seashell, agate, coral, amber, pearls, and other treasures, go out to sea and have their ships blown off course by a fierce wind to the land of the ogre demons, and if among them there is even a single person who calls the name of Regarder of the Cries of the World Bodhisattva, all those people will be saved from difficulties caused by the ogres. This is why the bodhisattva is named Regarder of the Cries of the World.

"Or if someone faced with immediate attack calls the name of Regarder of the Cries of the World Bodhisattva, the swords and clubs of the attackers will instantly break into pieces and they will be freed from the danger.

"Even if the three-thousand great thousandfold world were full of satyrs and ogres seeking to torment people, these evil spirits, hearing the people call the name of Regarder of the Cries of the World Bodhisattva, with their wicked eyes they would not even be able to see them, much less hurt them.

"If, moreover, someone, guilty or not guilty, is captured and put in stocks or manacles and chains, and they call the name of Regarder of the Cries of the World Bodhisattva, their bonds will be broken and they will be freed.

"Suppose a three-thousand great thousandfold world were full of vengeful thieves, and a caravan leader was guiding a group of merchants carrying costly treasures over a dangerous road. If just one among the merchants speaks out, saying, 'Good sons, do not be afraid. Wholeheartedly call the name of Regarder of the Cries of the World Bodhisattva, for this bodhisattva is able to give courage to all the living. If you invoke this bodhisattva's name, you will be freed from these vengeful thieves.' Hearing this, if all the traders together with one voice cry out, 'Praise to Regarder of the Cries of the World Bodhisattva,' by calling that name they will be freed from the danger.

"Inexhaustible Mind, such are the awesome divine powers of the great one, Regarder of the Cries of the World Bodhisattva.

"If any living beings are afflicted with a great deal of lust, let them keep in mind and revere Regarder of the Cries of the World Bodhisattva and they will be freed from their desire. If they have a great deal of anger and rage, let them keep in mind and revere Regarder of the Cries of the World Bodhisattva and they will be freed from their anger. If they are deluded by great folly, let them keep in mind and revere Regarder of the Cries of the World Bodhisattva and they will be freed from their stupidity.

"Inexhaustible Mind, Regarder of the Cries of the World Bodhisattva has such great divine powers and can abundantly benefit the living. Therefore all the living should constantly keep this bodhisattva in mind.

"Even if a woman wants to have a son and worships and makes offerings to Regarder of the Cries of the World Bodhisattva, she will bear a son blessed with merit, virtue, and wisdom. If she wants a daughter, she will bear one marked with beauty, one who had long before planted roots of virtue and will come to be cherished and respected by all.

"Inexhaustible Mind, such is the power of Regarder of the Cries of the World Bodhisattva. If anyone reveres and worships this bodhisattva, their happiness will not be neglected. Therefore, let all the living cherish the name of Regarder of the Cries of the World Bodhisattva.

"Inexhaustible Mind, suppose someone receives and embraces the names of as many bodhisattvas as there are sands in over six billion Ganges, and throughout their lives makes offerings to them of food, drink, clothing , bedding , and medicines. What do you think? Would such a good son or good daughter have abundant blessings or not?"

Inexhaustible Mind replied, "Extremely abundant, World-Honored One."

The Buddha said, "Suppose someone receives and embraces the name of Regarder of the Cries of the World Bodhisattva and just once worships and makes offerings to him. The blessings of these two people will be exactly the same, without any difference. They could never be exhausted in hundreds of thousands of billions of eons. Inexhaustible Mind, such is the immeasurable, unlimited merit and virtue one will obtain who receives and embraces the name of Regarder of the Cries of the World Bodhisattva."

Inexhaustible Mind Bodhisattva said to the Buddha: "World-Honored One, why does Regarder of the Cries of the World Bodhisattva travel around in this world? How does he teach the Dharma for the sake of the living? What sort of power of skillful means does he have?"

The Buddha replied to Inexhaustible Mind Bodhisattva, "Good son, if living beings in any land need someone in the body of a buddha in order to be saved, Regarder of the Cries of the World Bodhisattva appears as a buddha and teaches the Dharma for them.

"For those who need someone in the body of a pratyekabuddha in order to be saved, he appears as a pratyekabuddha and teaches the Dharma for them.

"For those who need someone in the body of a shravaka in order to be saved, he appears as a shravaka and teaches the Dharma for them.

"For those who need someone in the body of a Brahma king in order to be saved, he appears as a Brahma king and teaches the Dharma for them.

"For those who need someone in the body of Indra in order to be saved, he appears as Indra and teaches the Dharma for them.

"For those who need someone in the body of Ishvara in order to be saved, he appears as Ishvara and teaches the Dharma for them.

"For those who need someone in the body of Maha-Ishvara in order to be saved, he appears as Maha-Ishvara and teaches the Dharma for them.

"For those who need someone in the body of a great general of heaven in order to be saved, he appears as a great general of heaven and teaches the Dharma for them.

"For those who need someone in the body of Vaishravana in order to be saved, he appears as Vaishravana and teaches the Dharma for them.

"For those who need someone in the body of a lesser king in order to be saved, he appears as a lesser king and teaches the Dharma for them.

"For those who need someone in the body of an elder in order to be saved, he appears as an elder and teaches the Dharma for them.

"For those who need someone in the body of an ordinary citizen in order to be saved, he appears as an ordinary citizen and teaches the Dharma for them.

"For those who need someone in the body of a high official in order to be saved, he appears as a high official and teaches the Dharma for them.

"For those who need someone in the body of a brahman in order to be saved, he appears as a brahman and teaches the Dharma for them.

"For those who need someone in the body of a monk, nun, layman, or laywoman in order to be saved, he appears as a monk, nun, layman, or laywoman and teaches the Dharma for them.

"For those who need someone in the body of the wife of an elder, ordinary citizen, high official, or brahman in order to be saved, he appears as a wife and teaches the Dharma for them.

"For those who need someone in the body of a boy or girl in order to be saved, he appears as a boy or girl and teaches the Dharma for them.

"For those who need someone in the body of a heavenly being, dragon, satyr, centaur, asura, griffin, chimera, python, human, or nonhuman in order to be saved, he appears in such a body and teaches the Dharma for them.

"For those who need someone such as the god Diamond-Holder in order to be saved, he appears as the god Diamond-Holder and teaches the Dharma for them.

"Inexhaustible Mind, such are the blessings attained by this Regarder of the Cries of the World Bodhisattva and the various forms in which he travels around in many lands to save the living. This is why all of you should wholeheartedly make offerings to Regarder of the Cries of the World Bodhisattva. This Regarder of the Cries of the World Bodhisattva, this great one, is able to bestow freedom from fear on those who are faced with a frightening, urgent, or difficult situation. This is why in this world everyone gives him the name Bestower of Freedom from Fear."

Inexhaustible Mind Bodhisattva said to the Buddha, "World-Honored One, now I should make an offering to Regarder of the Cries of the World Bodhisattva." Then he took from his neck a necklace of many valuable gems worth a hundred thousand pieces of gold and presented it to him, saying, "Benevolent One, accept this necklace of valuable gems as a Dharma gift." But Regarder of the Cries of the World Bodhisattva would not accept it then. Again Inexhaustible Mind Bodhisattva said to Regarder of the Cries of the World Bodhisattva, "Benevolent One, out of sympathy for us, accept this necklace."

Then the Buddha said to Regarder of the Cries of the World Bodhisattva: "Out of sympathy for this Inexhaustible Mind Bodhisattva, for the four groups, and for the gods, dragons, satyrs, centaurs, asuras, griffins, chimeras, pythons, humans, nonhumans, and others, you should accept this necklace."

Then Regarder of the Cries of the World Bodhisattva, out of sympathy for the four groups, and for the gods, dragons, humans, nonhumans, and others, accepted the necklace, and dividing it into two parts, offered one part to Shakyamuni Buddha and the other to the stupa of Abundant Treasures Buddha.

"Inexhaustible Mind, freely using such sovereign divine powers, Regarder of the Cries of the World Bodhisattva travels about in this world."

Then Inexhaustible Mind Bodhisattva asked his question in verse:

World-Honored One of wonderful features,
Let me now ask you again,
Why is this buddha-son named
Regarder of the Cries of the World?

The Honored One with wonderful features answered Inexhaustible Mind in verse:

Listen to the actions of the Cry Regarder.
How well he responds in every region.
His great vow is as deep as the sea,
Unfathomable even after eons.

Serving many hundreds
Of billions of buddhas,
He has made a great pure vow.
Let me tell you briefly about it.

Those who listen to his name,
See his body, and keep him in mind,
Not wasting time,
Will be able to put an end to all their suffering.

If someone intending to harm you
Throws you into a burning pit,
Keep in mind the Cry Regarder's powers
And the pit of fire will become a pond!

Or if you are drifting around in a great ocean,
Threatened by dragons, fish, and various demons,
Keep in mind the Cry Regarder's powers
And you will not drown in the waves!

If you are on the peak of Sumeru
And someone pushes you off,
Keep in mind the Cry Regarder's powers
And you will stay in the sky like the sun!

Or if you are pursued by bad people
And thrown down from Diamond Mountain,
Keep in mind the Cry Regarder's powers
And not a hair will be injured!

If you are surrounded by robbers,
Each with a knife ready to use on you,
Keep in mind the Cry Regarder's powers
And their hearts will become compassionate!

Or if you get into trouble with the king
And are threatened with execution,

Keep in mind the Cry Regarder's powers
And the executioner's sword will break into pieces!

If you are imprisoned, shackled, and chained,
Your arms and legs in stocks,
Keep in mind the Cry Regarder's powers
And you will be freed from your bonds!

Or if someone tries to hurt you
With curses or poisons,
Keep in mind the Cry Regarder's powers
And the harm will revert to its originator.

Or if you meet evil ogres,
Poisonous dragons or various spirits,
Keep in mind the Cry Regarder's powers
And none of them will dare to harm you.

If you are surrounded by evil beasts,
With sharp tusks and frightening claws,
Keep in mind the Cry Regarder's powers
And they will flee in every direction.

If there are lizards, snakes, vipers, or scorpions
With poisonous breath that burns like fire,
Keep in mind the Cry Regarder's powers
And at the sound of your voice they will flee.

Or if clouds bring thunder and lightning flashes,
Hail pelts you, or rain pours down,
Keep in mind the Cry Regarder's powers
And all will instantly disappear.

If living beings suffer adversity
And are oppressed by countless pains,
The power of the wonderful wisdom of the Cry Regarder
Will liberate them from the world's suffering.

Perfect in divine powers,
Practicing wisdom of skillful means everywhere,
Throughout the universe there is no place
Where he does not appear.

All evil circumstances
In the realms of purgatories, hungry spirits, and animals,
In suffering birth, old age, sickness, and death—
Gradually he brings all of them to an end.

Hearing this from the Buddha, Inexhaustible Mind Bodhisattva joyfully said to the Buddha in verse:

True regarder, pure regarder,
Vast wisdom regarder,
Compassionate and kind regarder—
Always called upon, always looked up to!

His pure and spotless radiance
Is a wisdom-sun, destroying all kinds of darkness.
He subdues the storms and fires of disaster.
He illumines the whole world!

Precepts from his compassionate body shake like thunder.
His compassion is like a great cloud
Pouring Dharma rain like nectar,
Quenching the flames of affliction!

If you are brought before a judge in a dispute,
Or terrified in the midst of a battle,
Keep in mind the Cry Regarder's powers
And all vengeance will be driven away.

Wonderful voice, regarder of the cries of the world,
Brahma-voice, voice of the rolling tide,
World-surpassing voice—
He should always be kept in mind.

Never have a moment of doubt about him,
The pure and holy Regarder of the Cries of the World.
By those in suffering and agony, or facing death,
He can be relied on for protection.

Equipped with all blessings,
Viewing all with compassionate eyes,
His ocean of accumulated blessings is immeasurable.
Heads should be bowed to him.

Then the Bodhisattva Earth Holder rose from his seat, went before the Buddha, and said to him, "World-Honored One, if any living being hears this Bodhisattva Regarder of the Cries of the World chapter, hears of the freedom of his actions and the divine power of the revelation of the universal gateway, it should be known that this person's blessings are not few."

While the Buddha taught this chapter on the universal gateway, all eighty-four thousand living beings in the assembly became determined to reach the incomparable state of supreme awakening.

Appendix 2
Uchiyama Roshi's Postscript to the Kannon-gyo

When I, an ordinary man, encounter suffering, and I chant the name,
the life force that exists and actualizes within me, this is called Kanzeon.
Even though I don't perceive it, Kanzeon is functioning within me.
Therefore, I wholeheartedly chant the name.

When I, an ordinary man, feel like I am suffering,
I find that I don't understand the true meaning of suffering
Because I encounter different kinds of suffering and anxiety.
Therefore, I wholeheartedly chant the name.

When I, an ordinary man, feel like I am suffering,
Through the life of Kanzeon I can be delivered from suffering right now,
Because Kanzeon can instantly deliver me from suffering.
Therefore I wholeheartedly chant the name.

When this ordinary man is unable to call Kanzeon's name,
Because I call out Kanzeon's name, without knowing it
I wholeheartedly chant the name.

Appendix 3

Appreciating the Ten-Line Kannon-gyo[177]

The deepest meaning of the Kannon-gyo is contained in the short Ten-Line Kannon-gyo:[178]

> I take refuge in the Bodhisattva Kanzeon.[179]
> We have a causal connection with Buddha.
> We have a karmic affinity with Buddha.
> We have an affinity with the Buddha, Dharma, and Sangha.
> Permanent, blissful, self, and undefiled.[180]
> Every morning our thoughts are of Kanzeon.
> Every evening our thoughts are of Kanzeon.

177. The following commentary is based on a talk Uchiyama Roshi gave at Muryoji Temple in Nagano Prefecture in the summer of 1985.

178. Uchiyama Roshi refers to this work as the Ten-Line Kannon Sutra, but it is usually chanted in Buddhist temple services and is thought of as a short verse or hymn.

179. In Japanese this line is rendered as two lines, *Kanzeon / Namu Butsu*. This could also be translated as "Kanzeon, I pay homage to the Buddha."

180. Shohaku Okumura comments: Typically, the Buddha taught nonpermanence, suffering, nonself, and defiled, but just as Dogen said about the Heart Sutra, that is only half the truth: form is emptiness, emptiness is form but also form is form and emptiness is emptiness. We can't simply negate form and emptiness; that is only half the truth. It is not the Middle Way. We must actualize both form and emptiness. In the same way, we must actualize permanent, blissful, self, and undefiled along with impermanence, suffering, no-self, and defiled.

Thoughts continually arising from life.[181]
Thoughts not separated from life.

This short sutra, as it is used in Zen practice today, is well known to Japanese practitioners, who chant it regularly. For Japanese people, who have been chanting since ancient times, there are many chants that invoke various names, buddhas, or sutras, such as the nenbutsu (*Namu Amida Butsu*), *Namu Myo Ho Rengekyo*,[182] *Namu Shakamuni Butsu*,[183] *Namu Kie Sanbo*,[184] and *Namu Kanzeon Bosatsu*.

However, when we chant, for example, *Namandabu*, *Namandabu*[185] I think that often our minds wander, and we move our mouths out of habit while thinking about other things. At that point, some people might decide to put more effort into their chanting practice by choosing a more difficult sutra to chant so as to avoid just chanting mindlessly. You might think of chanting the Heart Sutra, for example, but maybe it is a bit too long and hard to remember. I think the Ten-Line Kannon-gyo is easier to memorize and more suitable for chanting.

The Ten-Line Kannon-gyo is a so-called apocryphal sutra composed in China sometime between the third and sixth centuries by members of the Nirvana School, which was a Chinese Buddhist sect based on the Nirvana Sutra. However, the substance of the Ten-Line Kannon-gyo is not at all apocryphal. Rather, it is the essence of Mahayana practice, and

181. Okumura Roshi's translation differs from the literal Japanese to reflect Uchiyama Roshi's interpretation. What would usually be translated as "mind" is here translated as "life." Instead of the usual Zen expression "Everything is mind," he is saying instead "Everything is our life"—or to use Uchiyama Roshi's expression, "Everything is the scenery of our lives."

182. Chanted by the Nichiren sects, including Soka Gakkai.

183. Referring to Gautama Buddha or Shakyamuni, the historical Buddha.

184. I take refuge in the Three Treasures: Buddha, Dharma, and Sangha.

185. A shortened version of *Namu Amida Butsu* that allows for easy repetition many times in quick succession.

it is truly wonderful. Just because a sutra was composed in India doesn't mean that it is the genuine article; conversely, sutras and other Buddhist works composed in China are not inauthentic. Works composed in Japan can also be authentic. The main point is, as long as the substance of the work teaches the essence of the Buddhadharma, then it is an authentic Buddhist work. Further, the Ten-Line Kannon-gyo, though short, truly teaches the deepest essence of Mahayana practice.

Having said this, even though we read the lines, we will certainly not quickly understand the deepest essence of Mahayana practice. More than likely, we might think that we can understand the words but then realize that we don't actually understand them at all. I think that most people understand only two of the lines: "Every morning our thoughts are on Kanzeon" and "Every evening our thoughts are on Kanzeon."

For me, the Kannon-gyo evokes a special memory of my first wife, who reminded me of the princess in the Japanese folktale, "The Tale of the Bamboo Cutter."[186] When I arrived at her sickbed, I didn't believe that she was going to die, but she herself had a premonition of her death. She said to me, "I want to continuously chant the Ten-Line Kannon-gyo, so please teach me the meaning." When I was a child, my mother chanted the full Kannon-gyo in front of the family altar every evening. Next, she would also repeatedly chant the Ten-Line Kannon-gyo. I had heard these verses since I was a child, so I knew them by heart, but I was completely unable to explain the meaning to my wife. At that time, I was twenty-four years old, and it has been exactly fifty years since then. Since I couldn't explain the meaning of this sutra to my wife, to make up for that, I wanted to spend the rest of my life reading Dogen's *Shobogenzo* and the New Testament, so I bought them both and gave them to her.

186. "Taketori Monogatari" is a sad tale of a mysterious and beautiful moon princess, Kaguya Hime, who is discovered by a bamboo cutter in the stalk of a glowing bamboo plant. She is raised as the only child of the bamboo cutter and his wife, but just when she comes of age and attracts many suitors, including the emperor, the people of the moon come to earth to reclaim her and take her back to the moon.

She was elated with my present and read from the *Shobogenzo* every day, especially the "Life and Death" chapter, and also diligently read the New Testament. Even though she couldn't understand it, she also chanted the Kannon-gyo until the day she died. She passed away on September 16, 1936.

I have been seeking the meaning of the Kannon-gyo ever since her death. It has been fifty years since she asked me to explain it to her, and I feel that I have at last grasped the heart of this teaching. I created a Japanese reading of the Chinese verses. I was not able to explain them to my princess, whom I bid farewell to fifty years ago, so I would instead like to explain them to you. I would be grateful if you could hear these verses with my sentiments in mind.

The thought that must be the great universe in the midst of the great universe[187]

What does the first verse, *Kanzeon Namu Butsu*, mean? Usually, it refers to the name of the Bodhisattva Kanzeon. Then *Kanzeon Namu Butsu* is usually read "Homage to Kanzeon" or "I pay homage to the Buddha Kanzeon." But I read it in Japanese as, "I see the sounds of the world and take refuge in the Buddha."

Having said that, Kanzeon Bosatsu was not an actual historical person and, in fact, the name Kanzeon itself presents problems. The Tiantai master Zhiyi, in his work "Profound Meaning of the Guanyin Chapter of the Lotus Sutra," wrote, "It is called contemplation because, after completely illuminating the true nature, we examine its root and branch. 'Sound of the world' is the object that is contemplated." Following Zhiyi, the expression usually has been rendered into Japanese as, "seeing the sounds of the world." But don't you think that "seeing the sounds of the world" is a strange expression? There are obviously a lot of sounds

187. Literally, the full heaven and earth.

in our world, and we hear them with our sense of hearing. However, in this expression, "seeing the sounds of the world," the word *seeing* is used. What does this mean? Doesn't *seeing* refer to our sense of sight or visual perception? How do you see a sound? Well, if you sit zazen you will understand. When you sit zazen, you use your eyes to look at the wall in front of you. The wall doesn't move at all. When you are sitting, all kinds of sounds come to your ears.

In the summertime, I spent some time in the town of Kiojiri in Nagano Prefecture at a retirement home built by my friend, Mr. Shimizu. Since he hadn't retired yet, he invited me to use the house to escape the worst of the summer heat in Kyoto. He has a wonderful teahouse on the grounds, and while I am there I always feel that I need to do zazen, so I sit every day. While I am sitting, the tranquil sound of flowing water running to the teahouse comes to my ears, and until the beginning of July I can hear the call of the cuckoo. However, the sound of the cuckoo's cry comes to my ears as an echo from afar in the mountains. At the same time, I can hear the sound of cars on a nearby highway. The sounds just enter my ears, but I don't make any effort to listen to them.

In this way, I can hear various sounds from the world as I sit without moving, but perhaps they are nothing but a kind of reflection or illumination. Therefore, how is this so-called hearing and seeing different from being illuminated? When we say we see, we are using our eyes and sense of sight, and when we hear we are using our ears and sense of hearing. Of course, there is an object that is seen and a sound that is heard. In other words, seeing and being seen and hearing and being heard are separating subject and object into two.

But in fact, the sound that comes to us when we are sitting zazen is before the distinction between seeing, being seen, hearing, and being heard—before the separation between subject and object. It is just a reflection or projection, an illumination. This is referred to as seeing. It is also referred to by the words *clearly seeing* or *eliminating and seeing*. For example, paraphrasing the Heart Sutra, "Avalokiteshvara Bodhisattva while practicing the deep practice of prajnaparamita looked upon the five skandhas and, seeing they were empty of self-existence, was delivered from all suffering." This is clearly seeing.

In other words, seeing and being seen and hearing and being heard don't happen after dividing our feelings and sense perceptions into two, but it is just living the reality of life before we divide things into two—before any discrimination, value judgment, or defilement. I'm always using the expression, "the reality of our life," but this reality of our life is not what we usually think of as our real life. Actual existence is before the division of seeing and being seen into subject and object.

The real reality of life is not the object that is seen, heard, or thought. It is the reality of life before the division into I and an object, before seeing and being seen, hearing and being heard, or thinking and being thought.

So now you are probably thinking, "Oh, I see, you must be talking about some state of mind or particular circumstance," some special mysterious place that I visit in zazen. But this is absolutely not the case. Here right now is the reality of life.

For example, living physiologically means breathing. However, we don't consciously breathe in each breath; we don't think about how much air we inhale or exhale. In other words, we are not thinking about breathing as an object while we breathe. We are just breathing. We just breathe from a place before the division into subject and object, before thinking and discrimination. However, when we take one or two deep breaths, we are conscious of that, starting with when we are born and take our first breaths and cry out. If we had to count how many breaths we have taken since then, I don't think anyone could do that. Even if we pull out our calculators, I don't think that we would be able to come up with a correct number.

In any case, when we are talking, eating, sleeping, and even thinking of something, we are breathing steadily. We are breathing before we begin to discriminate between subject and object. This is living the reality of life.

This is also true of the sounds of the world that come to us when we are doing zazen. My sounds? Or the sounds of the world? They are before the division into two, before duality, whether we think so or not, whether we believe it or not, whether we accept it or reject it, we are just sitting right here right now. This way of doing zazen is the Kanzeon of seeing the sounds of the world.

Zazen in the Tendai sect is referred to as *shikan.*[188] *Shikan* means opening the hand of thought and letting go and not chasing after thoughts as they come up—or, as Sawaki Roshi used to say, "Cease fire": just stop. We are letting go, but that doesn't mean that no thoughts come up. As long as we are alive, our mind is moving, so all kinds of thoughts keep popping up. But as long as we don't chase after them, they disappear like rootless weeds. Seeing means just letting the thoughts come and go and entrusting ourselves to just sitting as the thoughts appear and disappear. Since zazen is simultaneously ceasing and seeing, that is called shikan. Or, as it says in the Heart Sutra, "All five skandhas are empty."

Therefore, if we think that this seeing clearly represents some sort of mysterious, miraculous, or occult state, that is completely mistaken. We are living out reality, and for certain there is no special nirvana over there someplace. To use an example closer to home, it is dangerous to drive a car when you're preoccupied or upset. Also, drunk driving or falling asleep at the wheel is perilous. Don't drive like this but drive while first letting go of the hand of thought; you can't fall asleep, but you need to become fully awake, take in the scene moment by moment; all the places you come across are all the self, driving is at hand, flowing past. As long as you drive past these scenes, just as they are passing by you, if you take all of this as the self, you will drive safely. This is seeing. That is, "seeing the sounds of the world" is the essential attitude you should take when safely "driving" your life.

188. Literally, ceasing and seeing.

In the same vein, I have translated the first verse of the sutra as, "I see the sounds of the world and take refuge in the Buddha." The word *namu* means "to return to or take refuge in the universal life force." And *Butsu* is the reality of life prior to the dualistic separation into self and other. However, since we have conscious minds, we think many things and grab onto our thoughts and chase after them and, because of this, we leave the reality of our lives and float around in the air. For example, a thought suddenly floats into our head, and though this surely comes to us from the life force that pervades the universe, that thought, that judgment, happens when we separate self and other. When I try to make that thought into something that benefits me, then it ceases to be from the life force that pervades the entire universe. In other words, because this thought itself becomes the object of attention, we float away into space and become separated from the reality of the life force that pervades the entire universe. And from that place in space we create all sorts of problems for ourselves.

If we pause and open the hand of thought, we return to earth and to living the true reality of our lives. Whether we take refuge or not, the Buddha is the Buddha. Taking refuge in the Buddha or not, the reality of our life is the reality of our life. What is important now is surely that we need to return to the reality of our life right now. This is driving your life with the life of reality.

Since we possess a conscious mind, if we put it to work then surely we must learn how to return to the path of the reality of our lives. Instead, we use our minds for worthless things and lose sight of the true reality of our lives.

When I say this, you might think that returning to our lives is hard. But that's absolutely not true. I'm just saying that it's the natural thing.

In *Shobogenzo Genjokoan* ("Actualizing the Fundamental Point"), Dogen recounts the following story:

> Zen Master Baoche of Mt. Magu was waving a fan. A monk approached him and asked, "The nature of wind is ever present and permeates everywhere. Why are you waving a fan?"
>
> The master said, "You know only that the wind's nature is ever present—you don't know that it permeates everywhere."
>
> The monk said, "How does wind permeate everywhere?"
>
> The master just continued waving the fan.
>
> The monk bowed deeply.[189]

Zen Master Baoche was using a fan on a hot summer day. A monk came up to him and asked, "Air that is the substance of wind is found in the entire universe, isn't it? So why is the chief priest deliberately fanning himself? If you say that you must fan yourself for the wind to come, isn't that proof that you have not yet attained awakening?"

Then Master Baoche replied, "You only know that the wind's nature is ever present, but you don't know that it permeates everywhere." In other words, the monk was just showing off his limited understanding. Then the monk asked, "Then how does the wind permeate everywhere?" To which the master continued waving his fan.

Actually, the reason is simple and obvious. The wind that permeates the entire universe appears because we are fanning ourselves here and now, generating wind. If we just say that wind permeates the entire universe, if we don't fan ourselves, we won't generate wind. We are living the reality of our lives as the entire universe, but if we don't fan ourselves here right now, we will not manifest it as the wind of the reality of our lives as the entire universe. This is not especially difficult to understand; it's natural.

We human beings are stupid, don't you think? I mean, we think hard about this story about generating wind and how difficult this is to understand, but if we look at the facts, since we are in fact living the reality of

189. Okumura, *Realizing Genjōkōan*, 4–5.

life of the universe before dividing things into two, if we return to the facts of our life, the wind that permeates the entire universe is blowing. We just need to know this and return to our true lives.

On this point, what is important in terms of the Buddhist teachings is nothing more than "taking refuge in the Buddha." No matter whether it is Pure Land nenbutsu practice or zazen practice, the aim is to return to our life. Living our lives with this intention is what is meant by Buddhist practice.

If you don't drink with your own mouth, it's the same as not having a well spring of life.

I read the next section of verse in Japanese as "We have affinity with Buddha, we cannot escape from the Buddha, Dharma, and Sangha because we are connected."

As I said previously, the Ten-Line Kannon-gyo is thought to have been written by members of the Nirvana School in the Sui Dynasty (581–618 CE) and absorbed by the Tendai school. The Tendai tradition taught the teaching of the threefold buddha-nature, or buddha-nature as three causes. This term comes from the Nirvana Sutra, chapter 34, "On Bodhisattva Lion's Roar." In any case, as the seeds necessary for the attainment of Buddhahood, the three aspects of buddha-nature are (1) buddha-nature as the true cause, (2) buddha-nature as the revealed cause, and (3) buddha-nature as the conditions.[190]

Therefore, in my translation, "We have an affinity with Buddha," is equivalent to buddha-nature as the true cause; "we cannot escape from the Buddha" is equivalent to buddha-nature as the revealed cause; and

190. Buddha-nature as three causes: (1) the true cause, the principle of true reality that is inherent in all beings; (2) the revealed cause, the wisdom that sees that true reality is inherent in all beings; and (3) the conditions that help us to see that the true reality of all beings is within us.

"we cannot escape from the Buddha, Dharma and Sangha because we are connected" is equivalent to buddha-nature as the conditions.

"We have affinity with Buddha" means the original cause is the reality of life before cutting one into two. The reality of life is before anything arises in our minds. In other words, it is the reality of life before we discriminate between this and that; this is the fundamental cause. Therefore, this is buddha-nature as true cause.

Next, we say we are *connected* to the Buddha and are unable to sever this connection. This cause is the primary cause, but this alone is not connected to our realizing awakening. Buddha-nature as a *condition* is a secondary or subordinate cause and starts to relate to us as human beings. That means Shakyamuni Buddha awakened to the truth that we are all living out the reality of our life. As a result of his awakening, he understood that the reality of our lives is ourselves. The awakening that Shakyamuni experienced was absolutely not just his own awakening. When he attained awakening, he said, "I attained the Way together with the great earth and living beings—the mountains, rivers, grasses, and trees together all attained awakening." That is what the Buddha awakened to. In other words, since the Buddha already attained awakening, we can understand that we are living the buddha-nature. This is called buddha-nature as the revealed cause: the wisdom that sees that the true reality is inherent in all beings.

To put it more simply, if this is the wellspring of life, if we don't know it, then for us it's the same as if it didn't exist. However, Shakyamuni Buddha taught that indeed this is the wellspring of life and starting right then and forevermore that becomes the strength in our lives. Illuminating this is what buddha-nature as the revealed cause means. We have a mind, and as long as we use our mind without dividing our lives into the duality of subject and object that is buddha-nature as the revealed cause.

Buddha-nature as the conditions corresponds to the conditions that help us to see that true reality of all beings is within us. In our example, within ourselves the fundamental wellspring of our lives is gushing out. However, if we don't know this, it is the same as if it didn't exist. Shakyamuni awakened to this and discovered "the water of life is here." He completely revealed to us the existence of this water of life. This is the meaning of "we have affinity with the Buddha." We need to actually drink of this water or, said in another way, we need to fan our life with the wind of the universe. This is what is meant by "We have affinity with the Buddha; we cannot escape from the Buddha, Dharma, and Sangha because we are connected."

This means buddha-nature as a condition that helps us see true reality leads to comprehending buddha-nature as the true cause—the principle of true reality that is inherent in all beings. The Buddha, Dharma, and Sangha are the so-called Three Treasures of Buddhism. Japanese people these days mostly understand the first two treasures, the Buddha and the Dharma, but they might not understand the third, the Sangha. I understand the reason for this. Many Buddhist priests up until now haven't behaved in a manner that is worthy of respect. So, when we talk about the sangha as a treasure we surely feel embarrassed. However, in reality, the Buddhist sangha is necessary in order to activate the treasures of the Buddha and the Dharma. Just saying that in the past the sangha did not work hard enough and that the future of the sangha is hopeless is a childish way of thinking about the issue. Since Buddhist priests of the past were useless, then we need to say, "Okay, I'll change that." That is an adult way of thinking. In fact, although many Buddhist priests today agree that priests in former times were indeed useless, many of them decide to be useless too. But if these priests truly find their connection to the Buddhadharma and to the treasure of the Buddhist sangha, they can bring the Buddhadharma back to life. This is the intention contained in the verse of this sutra, "We have affinity with Buddha, we cannot escape from the Buddha, Dharma, and Sangha because we are connected."

The next phrase is "Permanent, blissful, self, and undefiled." I want to say that I am here right now wholeheartedly fanning the wind of the life of the entire universe.

Most people think that the Buddhist religion teaches impermanence. Certainly, early Indian Buddhism taught, "The world is impermanent; the world is suffering; there is no self that exists in the world; the world is defiled." All Buddhists have heard this, and I think that most people understand the teachings in this way.

For example, people think if they set aside money right now, they will be okay in their final years. But the world is impermanent, so no matter how much you're able to put away, the value of money itself is always decreasing. Even if you think about saving a million dollars toward your retirement, that one million won't be enough. That substantial amount changes in value, and before long, who knows, a pack of cigarettes might cost a million dollars. Young people might think that this is a ridiculous example, but the reality is that before the war, fifty dollars was a small fortune. Nowadays even a poor monk like me has fifty dollars. We can't rely on savings for our old age.

Further, if you think that the world is a fun place—it is not. For example, a small bird seems to be happily singing, but there is a line in a sutra about a bird chirping weakly because it is suffering. A skylark might be chirping, but it is defending its territory with all its might. So we might think that the skylark is enjoying singing, but actually it is suffering.

Or consider that we might think that we have a fixed self. In reality, our self is like a cloud that will disappear in an instant, so we teach no-self. We might think that the self is undefiled, clean, but we teach that it is not clean. Sooner or later, we are taught that what we obsess about is not true. Instead, we are taught impermanence, suffering, no-self, and impurity. But in the end these teachings are just expedient or skillful means of teaching the Dharma.

Neither teaching is the true Buddhadharma. When we say permanence and impermanence, suffering and joy, self and no-self, defiled and undefiled, these concepts are dualistic thinking, so this is not real Buddhadharma. The reality of life is before the division into subject and object. The reality of life goes beyond both permanence and impermanence.

When we breathe, we breathe and live; this is the reality of life. If we stop breathing, this cessation of breath is the reality of life. Therefore, this goes beyond permanence and impermanence. Nothing going in and nothing coming out—beyond permanence and impermanence is true permanence. In the same way, going beyond suffering and joy is true joy. Going beyond self and no-self is true self. Going beyond pure and defiled is true purity.

In other words, the verse "permanent, blissful, self, and undefiled"[191] is before we divide one into two; it is the reality of life before entering and departing. And so here also, should we translate this verse as "permanent, blissful, self, and undefiled," or take it a step further and say that I am here right now wholeheartedly fanning the wind of the life of the entire universe and, including that meaning, translate this verse as I have, "permanent, blissful, self, and impure"?

To the departed who died in the crash of Japan Airlines flight 123[192]

"Every morning we chant the sound that sees the world. Every evening we chant the sound that sees the world." What is important about this verse is taking refuge in the Buddha or returning to life. However, it's not good

191. This is in opposition to the Buddha's original teachings of impermanence, suffering, no-self, and defilement. However, as Uchiyama Roshi pointed out in the previous paragraphs, we need to be careful not to engage in dualistic thinking and just live life as the reality of our lives as everything we encounter is our life.

192. This refers to the tragic crash of Japan Airlines flight 123 in 1985. A faulty repair of the plane caused a bulkhead to fail, resulting in a rapid cabin decompression that ripped off a large portion of the tail, causing the loss of hydraulic controls. The pilots were unable to regain control of the aircraft. It is the deadliest single-aircraft accident in aviation history, in which 524 people lost their lives after the plane became uncontrollable and eventually crashed into a mountainside. The time between the damage to the aircraft and the crash was a bit less than an hour, so for that period of time the passengers had to face the fact that they would almost certainly die. Only four people survived.

enough simply to chant these expressions "take refuge" or "returning to life" one time. We have to chant them with each breath right now. We have to return to our life right now. Do not listen to talk about attaining satori in one shot. This is just a fairy tale and useless talk. It seems to me that Buddhists these days don't say this clearly enough. Buddhism itself is accepted as an already fully formed religion, but that is because it is not considered as the foundation of our lives. For me, it seems that these Buddhists are not always thinking about themselves as living, but instead only thinking about Buddhism as something based on boring myths.

Truly living fully and vigorously, we just breathe with each breath, always taking refuge in the Buddha, and return to life by taking refuge in the Buddha. This returning to life again and again we do continuously hundreds of thousands of times. That is what is meant by arousing bodhi mind: always completely renewing this attitude and setting out again with a fresh start. Rev. Doyu Ozawa[193] said, "Today, right now is my birthday." This act of renewal and making a fresh start is what is meant by "Every morning we chant and every evening we chant."

Recently, I was on a TV broadcast titled *Old but Not Old, Dead but Not Dead*. I said that I would send a copy of my book, *Life and Death: Selected Dharma Poems,* to anyone who requested it. Responding to requests, we sent out about four thousand copies. After a repeat broadcast, we sent out another two thousand copies. In any case, my assistant, Shusoku-san, and his group took care of this for me, so I didn't need to do it myself. However, he forwarded about ten letters to me. I was astonished by one of those letters. A woman sent me her family genealogy going back three generations. This genealogy contained fifty names and

193. Rev. Doyu Ozawa was a Soto Zen priest. As a young soldier in World War II, he lost both his legs. After the war, he experienced many difficulties due to his disability. After all his struggles, he made up his mind to believe that he was born just now, without legs. That was how he could accept the reality of his life at any given moment and live positively without his legs. He wrote a bestselling book about his experiences, *Today, Right Now Is My Birthday*.

ages, and after each name the woman had written the person's assorted problems and troubles, and she asked me what I thought she should do about them.

I took a deep breath and read her letter several times. She was the eldest daughter, and both her parents had died when she was young. As the eldest daughter, she became the de-facto parent and took care of her younger siblings. However, she was now in her sixties and her siblings were all getting older, with the youngest over fifty. All of her siblings had spouses and children, and the three-generation genealogy in her letter included her siblings' spouses, children, and grandchildren. She was worried about all those relatives' problems and asked my advice for each one. Reading this, I was filled with admiration and realized that a woman's suffering never ends.

I then wrote a response. I pointed out that her brothers and sisters were all over fifty, and that all of their children were on their own. All were adults, and all would be annoyed by her worrying and wouldn't listen to her advice anyway. I wrote that only they themselves could live their own lives, and it was now their responsibility to improve their lot. I asked her, "At this point, don't you think that it would now be best for you to reclaim your own life?"

Why am I talking about this right now? Because I want to say, my, how people let their thoughts float up into space! As for the woman who wrote to me, all of her siblings are troubled, and they all think that this is reality. If these folks were two or three years old, then she would need to worry, but worrying about these adults is excessive and is like departing from reality, floating in space. We should open the hand of thought and return to true reality and eventually return to the self that exists before separation into two. Rather than worrying about others, we must first live our own lives fully.

Many people come to me directly or write letters seeking my advice. As I listen to their problems, I take on all these troubles as my own. I don't think, "This has nothing to do with me." I contemplate how I would resolve the problem, engaging in a monologue with myself, and I give my answer. I don't really know how people who have come to consult me will receive my answer. I am just living the self, which is only the self, but this self which is only the self is this all-encompassing life that I meet. However, it is all-encompassing for me, but it is not the reality of life of the self of the other person. The reality of life is like this. It is important to return again and again to this reality of life.

Next, about Kanzeon. As for taking refuge in Kanzeon (*Kanzeon Namu Butsu*), in the past I read it as, "seeing the sounds of the world," but here I translated it as, "the sound that sees the world." We are always asking ourselves, "What should I do?" and grabbing onto this or that, losing our way. Through chanting *Namu Kanzeon*, we let go of the hand of thought. In the case of zazen, when we think in our heads about letting go of thought, that thought is not letting go of thought. We are just pulling our thought around like the cushion we are sitting on, and we're trying to push aside this thought like our cushion. That's not correct. Zazen is the posture of letting go of thought. It is a pose that we maintain with our flesh and bones, and completely entrust ourselves to it.

In the same way, when we are not able to do zazen and instead chant *Namu Kanzeon*, amid this sound of chanting *Namu Kanzeon* we let go of the hand of thought. Chanting *Namu Amida Butsu* or *Namu Kanzeon Bosatsu* produces the sound that sees the world, and we divert our minds from chasing after thought. If you're a Christian, praising God by singing a hymn, you divert your thoughts from the flesh. As it's a hymn, it is also seeing the sounds of the world. In either Christianity or Buddhism, if we speak from the point of view of the mystery of true religion, there are no differences.

The word *nen* in *nenbutsu* literally means idea or thought and indicates something one always remembers; it's in our memory, and we can't forget. So, whenever we remember it, we return anew to the reality of life; we let go of the hand of thought again and again.

Every thought arises from mind. Every thought is not different from mind.

Above, the word *mind* appears, and when we say mind, everyone these days assumes we mean something psychological. However, in the case of Buddhism, there are times when *mind* is used in the psychological sense, but in most cases not. Rather, most of the time it would be more accurate to translate the word *mind* into modern language as *life*. However, it doesn't by any means mean simply life in the physiological sense, but rather it means the reality of life before separating one into two or distinguishing between subject and object. Dogen said in *Shobogenzo Sokushinzebutsu* ("Mind Itself Is Buddha"), "The mind that has been authentically transmitted is 'one mind is all dharmas; all dharmas are one mind.'"[194] This is the Buddhist definition of mind. Put simply, it is the reality of life before we divide our lives and the Dharma into two separate things. Whether we think so or not, believe it or not, accept it or reject it, we are living out the actual reality of life hour by hour and moment by moment. And so, we are continually lived by our life, and we can't get beyond our life. If I say that I can't accept that, or if I try to deny it, just that very thought has floated up from the reality of life before being divided into two.

Poem Inspired by Psalms

Where can I go to be apart from Life?
Where can I go to escape from Life?
Even when I said, "I am greatly afflicted,"
I kept my faith in Life.
I venerate only Life.
I stay in stillness in Life.
That which makes me lie down in peace is Life.

194. Unpublished translation by Shohaku Okumura.

When you read this, you might think, "What a beautiful classical Japanese poem Kosho Uchiyama has created." However, this is just taken from passages that I really like from the Book of Psalms: 139:7, 116:10, 46:10 and 4:8. What I want to say is that the Hebrew Bible is mostly associated with the Jewish religion but is also related to Christianity. It is also a poem about the Buddhist teaching of the Buddha's life, and this sentence from Dogen's *Shobogenzo Shoji* ("Life and Death"): "This present life-and-death is the life of buddha."[195] Each of us just chant to the sacred life of the Buddha. We cannot lose this sacred life of the Buddha working through the self. When we are able to turn toward this true sacred life, we will truly come to understand it when I say that Judaism, Christianity, Buddhism, zazen, and nenbutsu are all the same. It is my sincere wish that I have been able to elucidate a little bit about the true religious life with my discussion of the Ten-Line Kannon-gyo.

195. Unpublished translation by Shohaku Okumura.

Bibliography

Braverman, Arthur. *Discovering the True Self: Kodo Sawaki's Art of Zen Meditation.* New York: Counterpoint Press, 2020.

Cleary, Thomas, trans. *Book of Serenity: One Hundred Zen Dialogues.* Boston: Shambhala Publications, 1998.

Dazhidu lun (Treatise on the Great Prajnaparamita). *Taisho Tripitaka* 1509.

Jungk, Robert. *Brighter Than a Thousand Suns: A Personal History of the Atomic Scientists.* Orlando, FL: Harcourt, 1958.

Kosho Uchiyama and Shohaku Okamura. *The Zen Teaching of Homeless Kodo*. Somerville, MA: Wisdom Publications, 2014.

Kosho Uchiyama Roshi. *Deepest Practice, Deepest Wisdom.* Translated by Daitsū Tom Wright and Shōhaku Okumura. Somerville, MA: Wisdom Publications, 2018.

———. *Opening the Hand of Thought: Foundations of Zen Buddhist Practice.* Somerville, MA: Wisdom Publications, 2004.

———. trans. *The Wholehearted Way: A Translation of Eihei Dogen's* Bendowa. Boston: Tuttle Publishing, 2011.

Leighton, Taigen Dan and Shohaku Okumura. *Dōgen's Extensive Record: A Translation of the Eihei Kōroku.* Somerville, MA: Wisdom Publications, 2010.

Mu Soeng. *The Diamond Sutra: Transforming the Way We Perceive the World.* Somerville, MA: Wisdom Publications, 2000.

Red Pine. *The Diamond Sutra: The Perfection of Wisdom.* Berkeley, CA: Counterpoint Press, 2001.

———. *The Zen Teaching of Bodhidharma.* New York: North Point Press, 1987.

Reeves, Gene, trans. *The Lotus Sutra: A Contemporary Translation of a Buddhist Classic*. Somerville, MA: Wisdom Publications, 2008.

Shohaku Okumura. *Realizing Genjōkōan: The Key to Dōgen's Shōbōgenzō.* Somerville, MA: Wisdom Publications, 2010.

Tanahashi, Kazuaki, ed. *Enlightenment Unfolds: The Essential Teachings of Zen Master Dogen*. Boston: Shambala Publications, 1999

———. *Treasury of the True Dharma Eye.* Boston: Shambhala Publications, 2010.

Watson, Burton, trans. *The Lotus Sutra*. New York: Columbia University Press, 1993.

Weinstein, Stanley, trans. "Treasury of the Eye of the True Dharma Book 28." *Dharma Eye* 10 (May 2002): 15–22.

Ziporyn, Brook, trans. *Zhuangzi: The Complete Writings.* Indianapolis: Hackett, 2020.

Index

H

I

J

K

O

P

R

S

T

U

V

W

X

Y

Z

About the Author and Translator

Kosho Uchiyama was born in Tokyo in 1912. He received a master's degree in Western philosophy at Waseda University in 1937 and became a Zen priest three years later under Kodo Sawaki Roshi. Upon Sawaki's death in 1965, he became abbot of Antaiji, a temple and monastery then located on the outskirts of Kyoto. Uchiyama Roshi developed the practice at Antaiji and occasionally traveled in Japan, lecturing and leading sesshins. The three pillars of his practice were his writings, his time spent guiding and talking with disciples and visitors, and zazen, the sitting practice itself. He retired from Antaiji in 1975 and lived with his wife at Noke-in, a small temple outside Kyoto, where he continued to write, publish, and meet with the many people who found their way to his door, until his death in 1998. He wrote over twenty books on Zen, including translations of Dogen Zenji in modern Japanese with commentaries, a few of which are available in English, as are various shorter essays. He was an origami master as well as a Zen master and published several books on origami.

Howard Lazzarini holds a bachelor's degree in Japanese language and literature from the University of California at Berkeley. He lived in Kyoto, Japan for twelve years, where he was a full-time lecturer at Doshisha Women's College. Also, while in Kyoto he studied with the Soto Zen master Kosho Uchiyama Roshi, practicing at his temple, Antaiji, in the north of city. After returning to the United States, he studied with

Shohaku Okumura Roshi at Sanshinji Zen Community in Bloomington, Indiana, where he took lay ordination as a student and follower of Zen Master Dogen Zenji and Shohaku Okumura Roshi. He also co-founded the Everett Zazen Group in Washington state in 2019 to practice with others in the Soto Zen tradition of his teachers. His wife, Shoko Hayashi Lazzarini, worked closely with him in the translation of this work and should be considered to be a co-translator.

What to Read Next from Wisdom Publications

Do Not Try to Become a Buddha
Practicing Zen Right Where You Are
Myozan Ian Kilroy

"*Do Not Try to Become a Buddha* is a grounded and refreshing exploration of the awakening path. Myozan reminds us to never separate from the people, landscape, and spiritual imagination. We embody looking, feeling and experiencing to be where we are and nowhere else. What could be better than always practicing in relationship with a courageous intimacy that serves others? Get this gorgeous book." —Koshin Paley Ellison, Zen teacher and author of *Untangled: Walking the Eightfold Path to Clarity, Courage, and Compassion*

Inside the Flower Garland Sutra
Huayan Buddhism and the Modern World
Ben Connelly

"Ben Connelly's contemporary commentary on thirty verses of a Huayan classic brings the profundity of an ancient tradition right into the palm of our hands. It skillfully evokes awe with the interconnectedness of everything in magical display, illuminating this very moment."—Judith Simmer-Brown, Naropa University and author of *Dakini's Warm Breath: The Feminine Principle in Tibetan Buddhism*

Inside the Grass Hut
Living Shitou's Classic Zen Poem
Ben Connelly

Enter the mind and practice of Zen: apply the insights of one of Zen's classic poems to your life—here and now.

Opening the Hand of Thought
Foundations of Zen Buddhist Practice
Kosho Uchiyama

"If you read one book on Zen this year, this should be that book."—James Ishmael Ford, head teacher, Boundless Way Zen, and author of *If You're Lucky, Your Heart Will Break*

The Zen Teaching of Homeless Kodo
Shohaku Okumura
Kosho Uchiyama

"Kodo Sawaki was straight-to-the-point, irreverent, and deeply insightful—and one of the most influential Zen teachers for us in the West. I'm very happy to see this book."—Brad Warner, author of *Hardcore Zen*

Deepest Practice, Deepest Wisdom
Three Fascicles from Shobogenzo with Commentary
Kosho Uchiyama

"Real Dharma. The mingled voices of these teachers—inspiring, challenging, sage, and earthy—shake dust from the mind so we may see more clearly what's right here."—Ben Connelly, author of *Inside Vasubandhu's Yogacara: A Practitioner's Guide*

About Wisdom Publications

Wisdom Publications is the leading publisher of classic and contemporary Buddhist books and practical works on mindfulness. To learn more about us or to explore our other books, please visit our website at wisdom.org or contact us at the address below.

Wisdom Publications
132 Perry Street
New York, NY 10014 USA

We are a 501(c)(3) organization, and donations in support of our mission are tax deductible.

Wisdom Publications is affiliated with the Foundation for the Preservation of the Mahayana Tradition (FPMT).